HOW TO MAKE MODEL SOLDIERS

written and photographed by
PHILIP O. STEARNS

HAMLYN
London
New York
Sydney
Toronto

Published by
The Hamlyn Publishing Group Limited
London · New York · Sydney · Toronto
Astronaut House, Feltham, Middlesex, England

ISBN 0 600 34857 1

Text setting and mono reproduction
by Tradespools Ltd, Frome, Somerset
Colour reproduction
by Wensum Graphics Limited, Fakenham, Norfolk
Printed by Cox and Wyman Limited, Fakenham, Norfolk

Contents

Introduction 4

1 A Brief History 6

2 Modelling Equipment 11

3 Assembly 15

4 Animation and Conversion 19

5 Sculpting and Casting 34

6 Painting 38

7 Dioramas and Scenery 58

8 Care and Display 68

9 Research 72

10 List of Manufacturers 76

Acknowledgments 79

Index 80

Introduction

It is but a few years since the ardent addicts of 'toy soldiers' were a small band, considered by their friends and acquaintances to be 'nutcases' – either a wee bit mentally retarded or just sincere eccentrics. Today military modelling and collecting societies are mushrooming at an unbelievable rate and their membership is merely the visible tip of an immense expanding iceberg of devotees to this fascinating and rewarding hobby. The toy soldier is now dignified with the title 'military miniature' (a touch of snobbery perhaps, but it does serve to elevate and distinguish its object from the genuine toy soldier). Whatever the term used, the subject offers an interest to anyone of any age, from the very young to the very old, and in any walk of life, with little restriction on the pocket book.

The adult enthusiast can 'catch the bug' in a variety of different ways. Possibly the most frequent is the renaissance of a long-forgotten boyhood addiction to playing with toy soldiers: to many a collector the present-day miniature is an adult toy whose sophisticated perfection reawakens in him the hours of pleasure he derived from the military toys of his youth. A chance visit to any one of the excellent military museums which have collections of figures and dioramas of a very high standard may equally well do the trick. As can a friendship with an ardent collector who is only too keen to expound on the joys of his hobby, or perhaps even taking one's child to a toy store where displays of high-quality military miniatures next to their less expensive brothers are very much on the increase. Even a casual visit to a hobby store may expose one to this highly contagious fever.

Once afflicted the victim is usually a hopeless case for life, but he will be giving himself an increasing scope for his own creative capabilities, finding a rewarding escape from some of life's more immediate problems, building associations with an international fraternity who will make him welcome in their homes and associate societies, increasing the depth of his historical knowledge, and creating for himself years of pure enjoyment and relaxation. To the really fortunate may also be added the zenith – the sharing and participation in his interest by one or more members of his immediate family. But to the long-suffering and patient 'model-soldier widows' I can only offer this consolation: count your blessings, ladies – it could be booze, girls, or gambling.

For the modeller there has never been a time when he has had such an immense choice of subject matter and quality of product offered to him in a market that seems to have no limit to its continuing expansion. Excellent kits can be found at prices well under a pound sterling or its equivalent in foreign currency. These rely entirely on the skill of the modeller to produce a finished product worth many pounds more to the pure collector.

There are enthusiasts who have neither the desire nor the talent to devote time to the assembling and painting of military figures. For them the only avenue open is the acquisition of a finished product. A wide variety of choice exists either through the stores specializing exclusively in militaria or by direct contact with the manufacturers who offer a finished painted service for their products, including the creation of little scenes and even dioramas to special order. There are also the bespoke artisans who work only on special commission and the many highly-talented amateur modellers who are often willing to part with their creations or make something up to meet one's personal specifications.

Both the bespoke artisan and his amateur counterpart are often hard to reach due to the increasing demand for their superb works. Thus to the pure collector the avenues open for the expansion of his personal collection lie mainly through commercial outlets specializing in the field and through personal contacts with other collectors and modellers. The only limitations on someone who remains purely a collector are personal taste and the size of his or her pocket book. To have a small collection including only the finest examples of the modeller's art is, to me, the ideal, but it must of necessity be a very expensive one indeed.

Strain on the family budget may finally force the collector to try his hand at modelling. Although his initial efforts may be frustrating and discouraging, with perseverance he will discover the modeller's pride in accomplishment, to say nothing of his fervent drive to improve technique. As an example, my personal collection is not a large one by any means, but it contains what I consider to be an example of the work of most of the finest artisans who have made military figurines to date. My own contributions to it are minimal – perhaps because they have suffered so by comparison to the masters – yet this has never deterred me for a moment from striving to emulate them to the utmost limits of my capabilities. This is why I urge the collector to try his hand at animating and painting, for not only will he derive a great deal of enjoyment from it, but it will also vastly increase his selectivity and acumen in judging the work of others.

Suffice it to say that be you a neophyte or an old hand at the game, be you a collector, modeller or both, you are a member of an immense international fraternity, a fraternity which will provide you with a full sense of enjoyment for the rest of your days. I can only hope that your participation in this marvellous hobby will benefit you with a host of international friends and exciting experiences as it has me.

Two Charles Stadden hussar figures from the firm of Norman Newton.

1 : A Brief History

In beginning any history of military modelling it is impossible to avoid what has now become the almost standard cliché – the citing of the famous Egyptian military figures, made in wood and found in the tomb of Prince Emsa at Assuit in Upper Egypt, dated roughly 2500 BC. Those little figurines represented the prince's guard and, as he was a well-known warrior, they accompanied him to his tomb as a part of his requirements for life in the hereafter. The real counterpart of these figures must have considered themselves fortunate by their representation in this manner; it was often the custom in those days for retainers, wives, and slaves to be buried alive with their masters.

For the next three thousand years, there seems to have been relatively little interest in military figurines. A few rare votive examples survive the Mediterranean and Middle Eastern civilizations. The Romans are known to have used a form of tin soldier for sand-table tactics, examples of which have been found at Magonza. Two tin figures of knights, dating from mediaeval times, may be seen at the Cluny Museum in Paris. However, these examples of what can be considered true model soldiers are so few and far between that they do not indicate the existence of representational armies. Then, in the fifteenth century, a number of armies were made in precious metals, primarily as the playthings of the European aristocracy.

By the seventeenth century, the art of warfare had become the interest not only of military leaders but also of men, and even women, in high and privileged positions. Children predestined by noble birth to become military leaders were often given miniature armies especially commissioned from jewellers or silversmiths. The most famous of these was that given by Queen Marie de Medici to her son, the future Louis XIII of France, and later inherited by Louis XIV. This army was made entirely of silver and was subsequently melted down during a period of dire strain on the Sun King's royal coffers. Also popular in these times were hand-painted cut-out military toys, but all such figures remained the privilege of the very wealthy until the end of the eighteenth century.

This knight in armour, made from tin and dating from the fourteenth century, was found during the dredging of the Seine. Height: 2¼ inches. Musée de Cluny, Paris.

With the breakthrough in metallurgy which introduced new alloys of tin, copper, antimony, etc., artisans were able to make available to the less privileged classes a whole range of items, among which were tin military miniatures. The invention of what is now referred to as the 'flat', or two-dimensional, figure is generally attributed to one Johan Gottfried Hilpert, who was born in Coburg in 1792, and in his hands was created the collector's miniature. He was the founder of a family tradition of model-soldier manufacture in Nuremburg which lasted for over one hundred years. Flats are still often referred to as 'Nuremburg' figures. However, in the records of the Nuremburg Guild of Pewterers there is evidence that this type of casting started as far back as 1578. Hilpert, nevertheless, is considered the first to devote his entire time to the production of military figures.

At the end of the eighteenth century, with the increasing standardization of military uniforms and the growth of professional armies as status symbols throughout Europe, came an increased public interest in things military. It was also at the end of this century that the solid or *ronde bosse* figure came into being, fathered by a French metal worker in Paris, one Lucotte. He started production in 1789 and reigned supreme in the field until about 1850, when several competitors challenged his position. Eventually the firm of Lucotte amalgamated with its competitors under the name of Mignot and the company remains to this day one of the largest manufacturers of *ronde bosse* figures in France, with a world-wide distribution.

Production of solid figures took a great step forward when in 1893 William Britain introduced a new method of hollow-casting model soldiers in Britain. This greatly reduced their cost and began placing them within the reach of the smallest purses. However, mass production lowered the quality and eventually led to a decline in interest in figures, even as toys, due mostly to the crudeness of the painting. The vast demands placed on all metal by World Wars I and II greatly reduced production of model soldiers, and the era between 1918 and the late 'forties constituted the dark ages in the world of the military miniature.

Solid lead soldiers made in France.
Left: **A *cuirassier à cheval* dating from the seventeenth century. Height 6½ inches. Musée de l'Armée, Paris.**
Right: **Playthings of the imperial princes of France. Height: 11½ inches. Musée National du Château de Compiègne, Compiègne.**

Top: **Lead flats, made in the United States and dating from the nineteenth century. The figures represent officers in the US Civil War, and that on the far right (labelled Hancock) may refer to a general in the Northern Army, Winfield Scott Hancock. Height: 2½ inches. Percy Band Toy Collection, Canada.**
Bottom: **This cross-section of modern flats (tin, 30mm) from the collection of Dr Alastair Bantock gives only the barest impression of the unlimited subject matter available today.**

The British Model Soldier Society, founded by a gallant few devotees in the early 'thirties, has maintained its interest principally in Britain products and today some of its members can field armies of many thousands of Britain soldiers. A box of eight figures on foot or five mounted which used to cost 10½d. (and, mind, I am not talking about new pence) now fetches prices in the high double figures and sometimes even three figures in pounds sterling. Britains

are now classified as antiques or curios and their value has skyrocketed, due, in part, to the firm ceasing to produce metal figures a few years back in favour of plastics. Today, anyone discovering a set of Britains in some long-forgotten corner of an attic or cellar can reasonably expect to acquire two pounds or more per figure if they are still in their original box. I, personally, cannot understand this mania in view of the incredibly high product standards of present-day firms catering to the military collector. However, God bless Mr Britain for what he has done for children from eight to eighty during these past years.

The year 1947 saw the renaissance of both interest in, and production of, model soldiers. Mignot in France and Elastolin in Germany began to re-emerge, and several new masters in 'flats' hit the market, along with such bespoke artisans as Berdou, Metayer, and the supreme artist of miniatures, Mademoiselle Josiane Desfontaine. In the beginning, collecting was slow to catch on, but by 1950 the hobby had begun to gain momentum and it has now become truly international, spawning many publications and societies throughout the world. It is big business for many manufacturers whose names are household words in the international modelling fraternity.

The British firm of Norman Newton, founded in 1953 with its superb master figure-maker, Charles Stadden, was more responsible for launching the modern quality *ronde bosse* figure at a reasonable price than any other, in my opinion. The merchandizing of its products was designed to attract the collector of finished figures, as well as the do-it-yourself painter, and it was the first to devote itself entirely to the collector's world on a semi-massproduction basis. Its ten-year start put it far ahead of more recent competitors. Today many of its former employees have set up competitive firms, and in the past ten years many small organizations creating superb figures have emerged internationally. Still, it cannot be denied that Newtons pioneered the serious aspects of model-soldier modelling as we know it today.

Top: **Ancient Britain cavalry figures in their original boxes. Today, in this condition, such figures will fetch extraordinary prices.**
Bottom: **Modern Britains are available in various lines in metal, plastic, or combinations of both.**

At the same time as interest in the model-soldier world was being reborn, some of the industrial giants in the toy field began devoting more of their production to military kits of aeroplanes, ships, military vehicles, and finally to appropriate companion figures. This particular kit industry did not fully emerge until the advent of plastic and its derivatives. The use of such materials in military modelling has been beneficial because it has once more brought the cost of military modelling within the range of any pocket. Moreover, plastic in the hands of serious quality manufacturers has made possible a standard of detail which in many instances far exceeds the possibilities in metal.

A pioneer in the field of serious collector figures was the firm of Historex in Paris. This firm brought together the outstanding talents of Maitre Eugène Lelievrepre, official artist to the French Army, and M. René Gillet, who created Historex as a subsidiary to his already flourishing commercial-engraving business. Historex has set a quality standard which has seldom been approached and the firm has done for plastic figures what Norman Newton did for metal collector figures.

So today, in the 'seventies, we have arrived at a stage when leisure pursuits are on the rapid increase, and military modelling has never enjoyed a greater popularity. A witness to this is the recent formation in America of a national chain of modelling supermarkets called The Squadron Shops, which cater exclusively to the modeller's needs. We have certainly come a long way from the day of the isolated 'nutcase' collector of toy soldiers.

Left: Stadden figures of the Frederick the Great period, superbly painted in a scene by Ronald Burgess.

Below: Some of the many scales of figures at present manufactured in metal. (*Left to right*) 54mm Stadden Miniatures; 54mm Phoenix Model Development; 90mm Men O'War; 15mm Miniature Figurines; 25mm Gilder/Hinchcliffe Models; 90mm Superior Models; 20mm Stadden Miniatures; 120mm Ray Lamb/Hinchcliffe Models; 30mm Stadden Miniatures; 77mm Series 77 Military Miniatures; 30mm flat (maker unknown); 75mm Ray Lamb/Hinchcliffe Models; 54mm Lassett Miniatures; 25mm Garrison Figures; 54mm Sanderson Miniatures; and 54mm Ensign Miniatures.

2: Modelling Equipment

Once you have contracted the military modelling disease it is almost impossible to remain simply a collector. The sheer pressure of all the superb miniatures available only in kit form today will inevitably drive you to try your hand at assembling and painting figures. No matter how limited your talents may be, the challenge of 'doing your own thing' will triumph in the end. Even though results may be a bit discouraging at first, if you persevere the huge satisfaction to be found in developing your own modelling techniques and the far greater enjoyment to be derived from a fuller participation in this marvellous hobby will soon dispel any such feelings. So let us now get down to the practical side of military modelling.

Below are the tools which will be essential to your life as a modeller. Fortunately they are neither too numerous nor expensive, but at this point let me offer a quick word of advice. Buying a few of the best and slightly more expensive tools at the outset will prove to be a wise economy in the long run. Therefore I recommend that you start by visiting a shop dealing in jeweller's supplies. Here you will find the best and most efficient tools for your hobby. Although most of these tools can be acquired in tool sets specifically manufactured for modellers by such firms as Exacto and Humbrol, I feel that the extra quality you will get from jeweller's tools far outweighs the small extra expense.

In addition to these, I should like to recommend a few non-essential but most valuable tools without which my modelling life would be purgatory. The first one is an instrument called a Pyrogravure, which is manufactured in France but distributed here and abroad through Historex agents. This engraving instrument with a

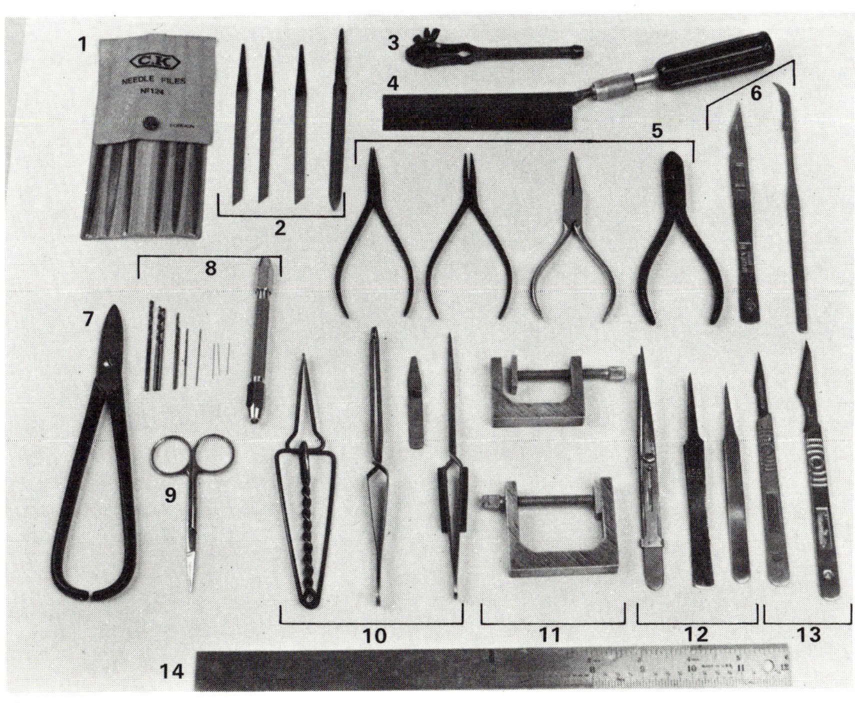

The essential modelling tools:

1 a set of needle files
2 a set of jeweller's engraving tools
3 a jeweller's hand-vice
4 a razor saw
5 a set of assorted jeweller's long-nosed pliers
6 two craft knives
7 jeweller's metal scissors
8 a multi-chucked pin-vice and assorted drills
9 nail scissors
10 a set of cross-clamp tweezers
11 a set of small C-clamps
12 a sharp-pointed and a round-nosed set of tweezers
13 more craft knives with assorted blades
14 a small steel rule

Right: **Helpful, but non-essential equipment from the jeweller's tool kit:**
1 an articulated clamp and stand
2 a magnifying glass
3 a combination bench-vice and hand-clamp
4 a hammer and anvil
5 a jig and clamps
6 a saw

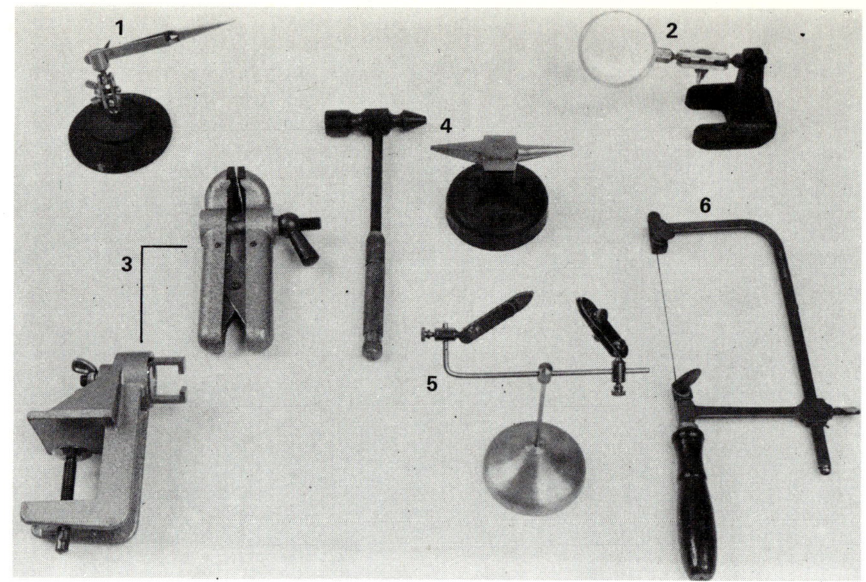

Below: **The Pyrogravure, an invaluable tool for manipulating, soldering, and fine-detailing polystyrene.**

variable-heat controller and assorted points is the ideal instrument for the converter working with polystyrene. Next I would recommend a jeweller's anvil and hammer; these are particularly useful when working with metal figures. Another discovery in the jeweller's tool bag is a small bench-vice which also acts separately as a hand-vice, and last but not least is a tool which can only be described as a jeweller's jig. It has two movable ball clamps on arms which can be positioned anywhere along the cross bar. If you are working on two separate pieces you wish to join together with a slow-drying bonding agent, this little gadget is a great boon for not only does it eliminate the trembling hands of advancing years, but it also

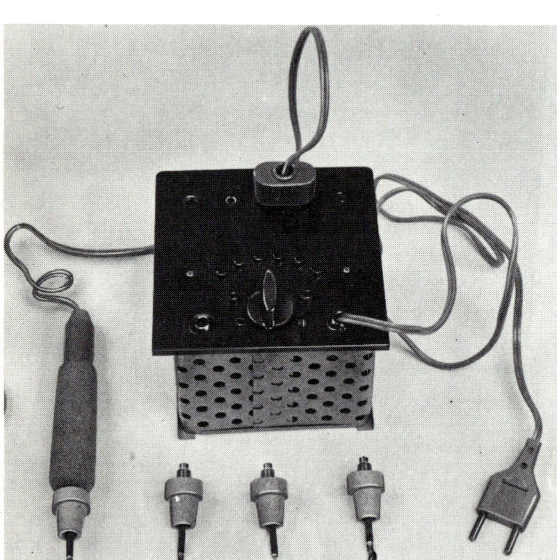

leaves you free for other work. Should you purchase one of these little gems I am sure you will keep discovering as many new uses for it every day as I do.

Now on to a list of the materials you should have on hand. I do not wish to mention too many brand-name products for some are available only in certain countries, but with a little research a modeller can find products similar to those I do list in his own locality. Most hobby stores can offer very good advice on this subject.

The most important of these materials are your *bonding agents*. With the advent of the space age there has emerged a plethora of new products and materials designed to withstand the rigours of space travel. Among these are bonding agents of various kinds which are a great boon to modellers.

The first I shall mention is a product called Permabond, and it is equally applicable to either metal or plastic. This extraordinary adhesive will bond metal parts together more firmly than soldering and it can be used on any material other than pure polythene. It also has the great advantage of being very economical in use – one drop will cover a square inch of bonding surface – and this offsets its relatively high cost. It needs only fingertip pressure for about twenty seconds to set. It is unaffected by extremes of heat or cold, and it requires no messy mixing as with various resin-based epoxys. I have found it to be the most efficient and economical bonding agent I have ever used, not only in modelling but in many other household uses. A word of warning, however:

Above: **Effective bonding and filling agents, plus a selection of micro-strip, rod, and sheet polystyrene (bought from modelling shops) and assorted sizes of fine fuse-wire for horses' ropes, cables, etc.**

Right: **Finally, a real luxury, an electrically-driven drill, with buffer and polishing attachments.**

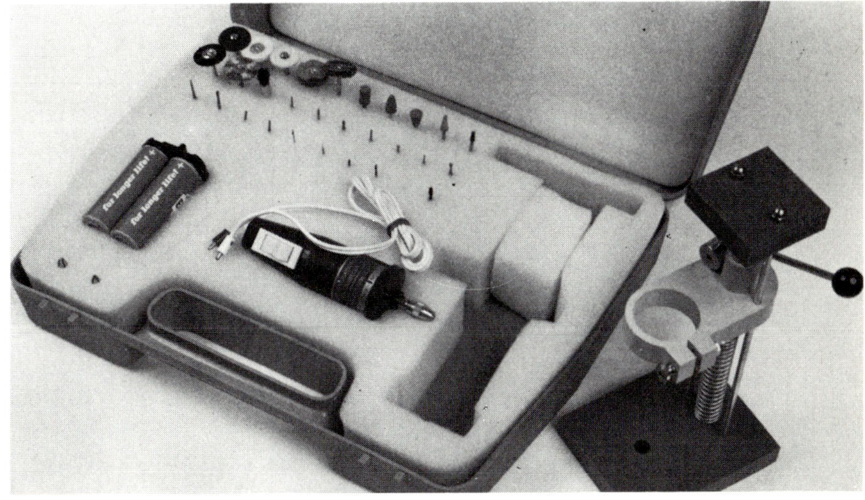

do not get it on your fingers or you may find them firmly stuck together or to one of the pieces you are trying to bond.

There are of course many other types of bonding agent available, most being based on a catalystic action between an epoxy and a hardener. A number of them are somewhat messy to use and each requires a different amount of time in which to set. Also very few will work equally well on metal and plastic. However, I have discovered one product, called Heatherbond Plasteel Putty, which is extremely useful as both a bonding and filling agent. It can be used almost like plasticine for modelling and it adheres equally well to both metal and plastic. Having a steel-powder base, it dries rock hard in twenty-four hours.

For the plastic modeller there are a number of excellent liquid and semi-liquid cements. However, I have found that liquid cement is quite sufficient for all requirements in plastic modelling and much cleaner and more efficient to use. The most effective can be acquired through your doctor for it is a chemical called dichloromethane. Remember this liquid must be kept in a green bottle firmly capped when not in use and stored in a dark corner. It has a chloroform base and therefore care should be taken when using it. However, there are a number of brand-name products, such as Mekpac, which are designed exclusively for modellers. These are almost as efficient and do not require any special care.

Very necessary to the plastic modeller are the *filling agents*. The best of these, I have found, is a product called Squadron Green Putty. It is available through Almark in England or direct from the Squadron shops in America.

One last addition to the requirements list: assorted packs of plastic cards, plastic strips, and plastic rods, essential in super-detailing figures. For metal conversions you can acquire empty oil-paint tubes, which are excellent for making cloaks, straps, belts, etc.

With your tools and materials at hand you are now ready to start assembling a figure. One quick word of advice about the working area you have selected. Make sure it is well lit, and that you have enough space to keep all your equipment neatly stored. Cover your working surface with a large blotter or stiff craft-paper which can be changed periodically and thus you will not ruin the surface of some treasured piece of furniture in the house. If you have your own work bench so much the better.

I cannot stress too heavily the necessity of cleaning and neatening your working area after each modelling session. The extra few minutes you take in restoring order will save you countless hours of frustration looking for tools or lost bits and pieces of your model. You will find that during a session your working surface becomes somewhat chaotic – this is only natural, but periodic restoration of order will greatly increase your efficiency as a modeller.

A tidy and well-organized working area has positive advantages for the military modeller. Devices like the spinning 'Lazy Susan' (*above*) make a contribution to efficiency, and note the plastic sandwich-covers used to alleviate dust problems (*right*).

3: Assembly

Metal

Let us assume you have elected to start work on a metal soldier kit. The first thing to remember when you open the box or pouch in which it is enclosed is that all the little bits and pieces should be emptied into an appropriate container so that nothing is lost.

Then check the castings for flash lines. These are the hair lines that are left on the casting where the two halves of the mould join together. Even the finest castings in either metal or plastic are subject to varying degrees of flashing. These flash lines should be carefully scraped away with either your craft knives or engraving tools and then smoothed down with a needle file. Nothing ruins a figure more thoroughly than evidence of join lines after it has been completed.

Now that you have cleaned all the elements of your casting, try assembling the pieces to check that they fit properly. Here you may find further filing and scraping necessary. When you are satisfied with the fit of all the pieces, a quick clean with a solution of household detergent and water – to get rid of any grease or dirt accumulated while handling – and you are ready for assembling.

It is at this point that you must consider how much of the figure you are going to assemble before priming and painting. An oft-expressed maxim to which I do not subscribe is: 'If you can see it, you can paint it.' It is a great mistake in my opinion to assemble a figure completely only to find that visible areas are impossible to reach with your paint brush. It is, for instance, quite obvious that with a hussar figure, where a great deal of detail is visible under his pelisse, it would be impossible to assemble him completely before painting. In this case you would paint the figure and the pelisse separately and do your final assembly afterwards.

Now you must make your choice of whether to solder, glue, or epoxy your figure. I find that for me soldering is very difficult to master, as witnessed by the disastrous dissolution of countless figures into lumps of metal. However, for many it is a happy choice. We will assume that you have settled for my favourite discovery, Permabond. You hold the first two pieces for bonding firmly in position with finger pressure and apply one sparing drop from the point of the container to the top of the seam of the pieces to be joined. Keep the pressure on for thirty seconds, and presto, your soldier's arm is wedded to his body forever. Assemble all the pieces required at this stage in a similar fashion.

Then examine your figure carefully to see if there are pock marks or seams that do not quite fit. If so, it is now that you take out your filler, in my case Heatherbond Plasteel, and add whatever is needed. It is a good idea to put on a tiny bit more filler than seems necessary because many fillers shrink slightly when fully cured.

Do not try to rush things in your enthusiasm to see your figure completed. Set it aside and give the bonding agents and fillers a chance to cure properly. When they have set and you have filed and smoothed the figure, you are ready to prime and paint.

The preparation and assembly of a horse kit follows essentially the same procedure. In as much as horses are composed of larger pieces, you may find you have considerably more filing to do around the various joins, and, here again, I must stress the importance of giving your bonding and filling agents plenty of time to set and cure before starting to file. A variety of horses can be achieved with great success using kits from manufacturers like Imrie-Riseley in metal or Historex in plastic. Both these firms offer a large number of choices in heads and half-body castings, most of which can be combined to create a wide range of horse poses. When preparing a cavalry figure do not join the rider, the saddle, and the horse until each of these items has been painted.

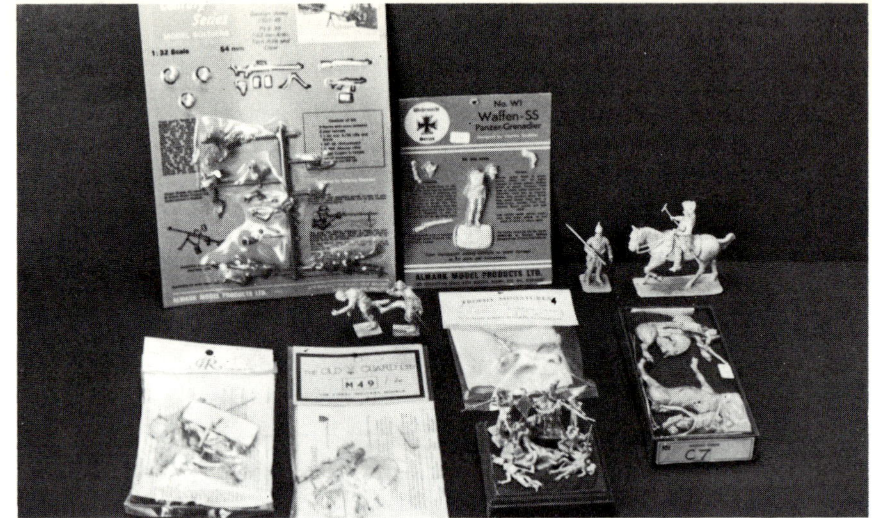

A good cross-section of the popular model-soldier market, showing how manufacturers package and present their products. All these figures are metal.

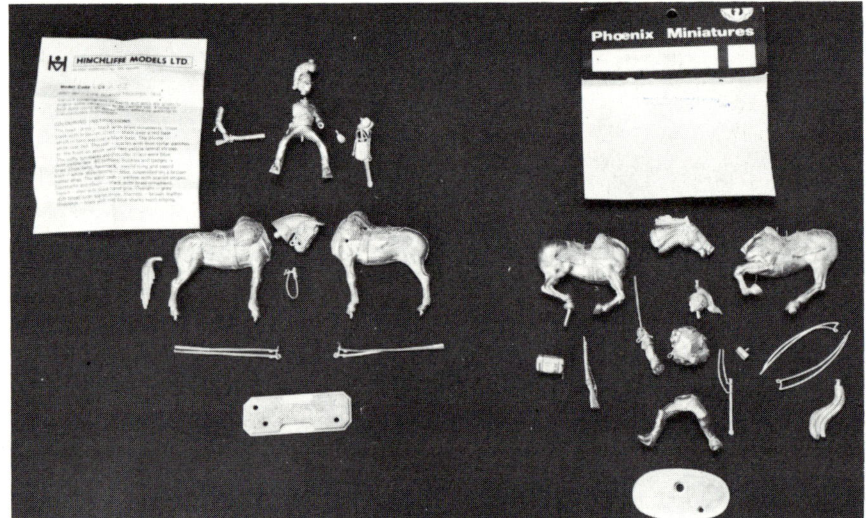

The contents of a Hinchcliffe and a Phoenix cavalry kit compared. Both models are metal.

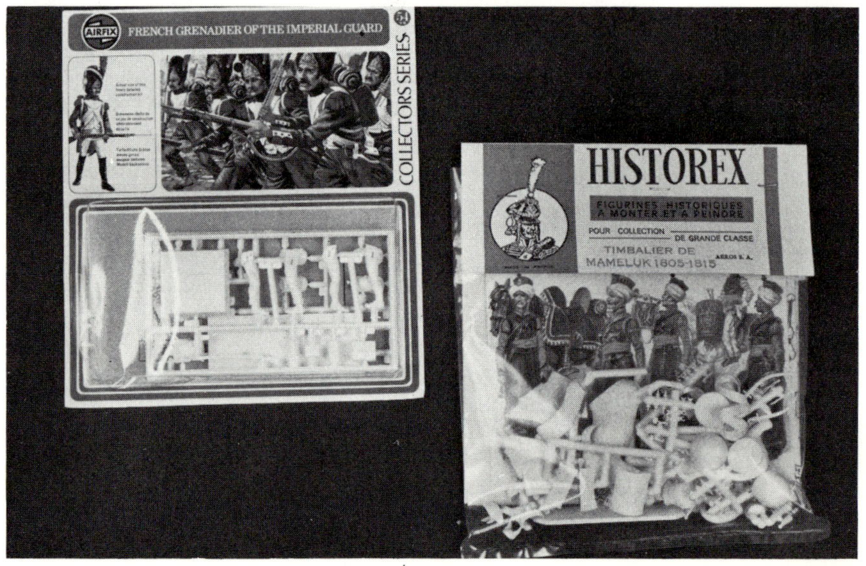

In contrast, these are the packaging methods of the plastic giants in the trade, Airfix and Historex.

Plastic

The assembly of plastic figures follows essentially the same procedure as with metal. However, plastic is far easier to clean and prepare, and the liquid cements dry and set far more rapidly.

Taking the best of the plastic military-miniature kits, Historex, you will at once find a plethora of tiny details all cast separately on sprues. It is here that extreme care must be taken in keeping all those fiddly bits carefully stored in your container. Do not remove a piece until you are ready to cement it in place. I cannot overstress the necessity of neatness and care when working with Historex kits so as not to lose any essential pieces when you are assembling figures. Remember the material is very light and the pieces very small and if you cough or sneeze at the wrong moment you are liable to lose a most necessary bit of detail. With care, however, you will find your Historex figure growing into a pure joy of precise and miniscule detail that you had not dreamed possible. These kits are far more difficult than is apparent when you first start, but with slow and patient care in assembling you will be delighted with the results.

The Airfix plastic collector-figure kits now appearing on the market are very good value for money though in my opinion they cannot compare with the amount of detailed pieces that Historex kits offer. However, the advantages that the Airfix kits have for the beginner are the instruction diagrams included in each kit and the numbering of each part of the figure on its sprue. A logical sequence can be learned from assembling an Airfix kit, which may assist in future assembling of more complicated kits.

A myriad tiny pieces comprise the Historex kit of a Mameluke kettle drummer. It is interesting to compare the number of pieces in this kit with those in the metal kits opposite.

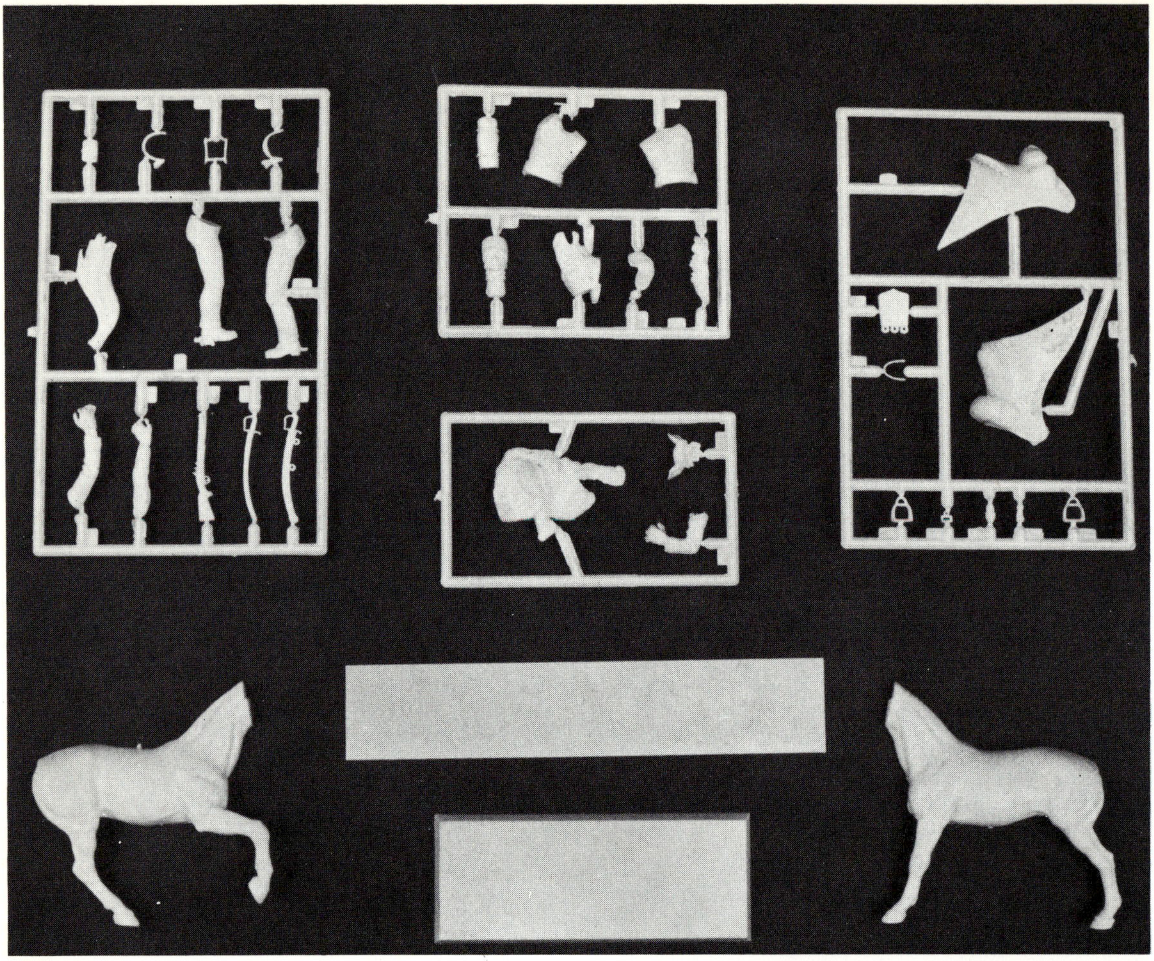

Above: The Airfix British hussar plastic kit with its neatly numbered pieces arranged on sprue sections.

Right: Historex offer a choice of six basic horse kits, but as can be readily seen all the head and body halves can be interchanged, giving an almost unlimited number of action poses.

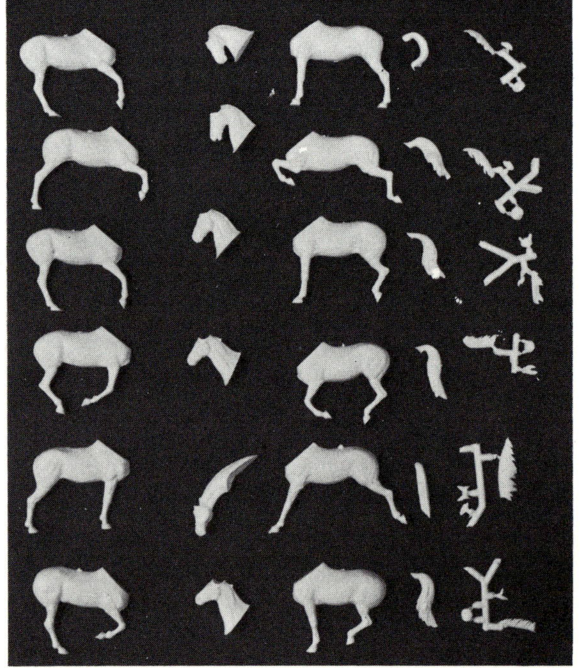

4: Animation and Conversion

So far we have been concerned with assembling either a metal or plastic figure as it comes from its package. The amount of work this requires will depend upon whose kit you select and the number of pieces contained in it. Let us assume that by now you have assembled and painted several standard figures and you feel the desire to be more adventurous and creative in your modelling. What avenues are open to you?

Essentially there are two. The first is animation and conversion. The second is sculpting and casting your own creations. Animation means imparting life and vitality to a stiffly posed figure by altering its pose. Conversion means adding to, or subtracting from, a standard figure to give it your own chosen individuality. You would be well advised to spend a great deal of time and effort on animating and converting existing figures before you begin to sculpt and cast your own, unless of course you have had a basic training in classical art and sculpture. Therefore I shall devote only a very small section to sculpting and casting, and concentrate mainly on the many possibilities offered by animation and conversion.

Metal

Let us start by animating a metal figure. Before animating any figure you must first consider very carefully what you want to do with it. At first it is wise to try out only the simplest ideas – like changing a pose.

Bending a metal arm or leg requires an incision at a major joint and the cutting away of a certain amount of the material to allow the bend to be completed. Say, for instance, the arm is straight down at the side of the figure and you wish to bend the elbow upwards. By taking your cutting pliers or one of your saws and making a V-notch on the inside of the arm at the elbow and then carefully and slowly bending the arm below the elbow, you can close the gap you have cut out, thus moving the arm upwards.

To a certain degree you can reverse this procedure to straighten out a limb but anatomically it is never quite as successful. The outside of the elbow is stretched and may look completely wrong, in which case you will have to replace the material you have cut from the inside of the arm by building up the elbow on the outside with an appropriate filler.

When animating, you must always consider the anatomical problems involved in changing poses. Go and have a look at yourself in the mirror and think how you are going to achieve the pose you wish to show in your model. Remember that bending or twisting limbs should be kept to a minimum for it tends to stretch the metal and makes it very brittle. With plastic you can cut limbs and bodies and fill them in or change sections completely, but this is well-nigh impossible with metal figures and you are far better off keeping your changes down to those which do not risk ruining an expensive metal casting.

1

1 To demonstrate metal animation, Graham Bickerton used a Series 77 mounted officer of the Napoleonic Polish Lancers by Pat Bird. On the right of the picture we see the figure as it is sold by the manufacturer. The animated painted figure is on the left. Obviously the latter greatly enhances what is a good basic figure.

2 The horse was sawn from the base and its tail removed. Next the reins and halter rope were cut from the casting with a craft knife, and the neck of the horse was partially severed where it joined the head.

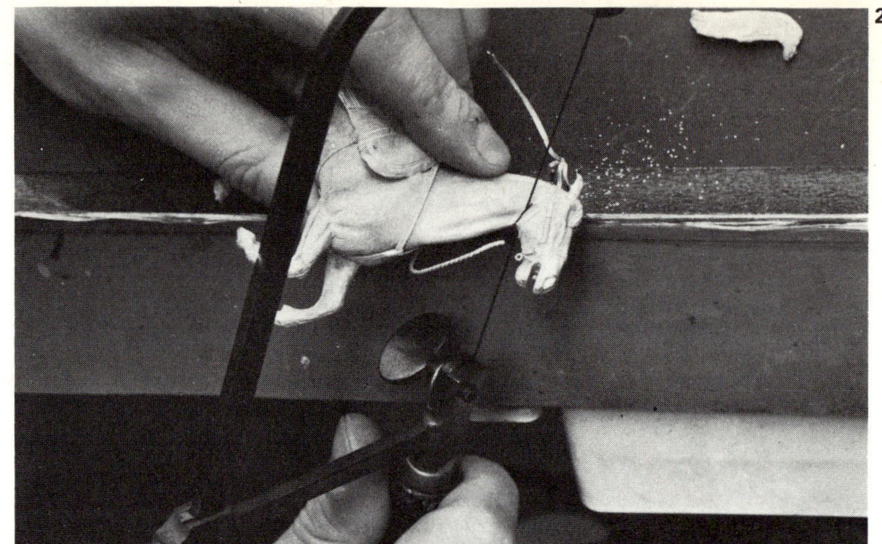

2

3 A V-shaped section of the throat was cut away to allow for the re-shaping of the throat with filler.

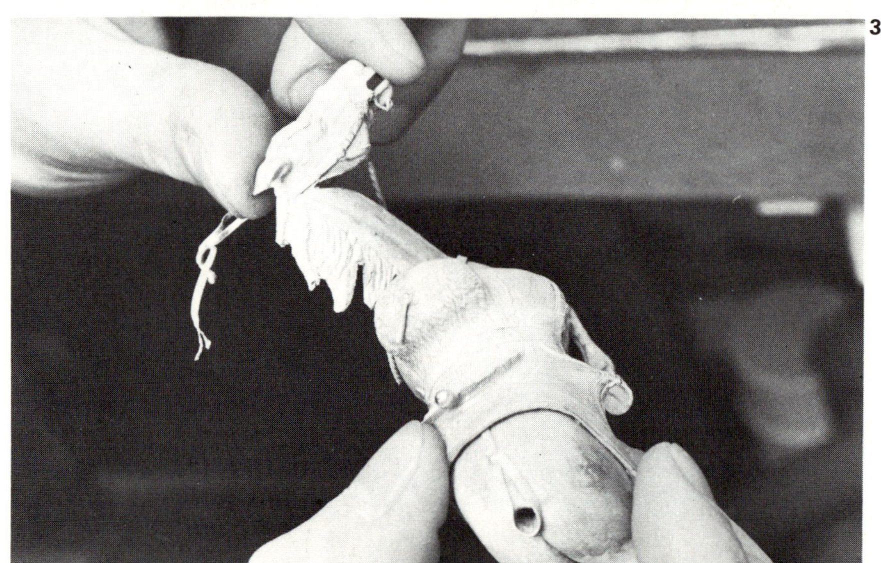

3

4 Then the head was slowly twisted and bent to the desired position while the figure was held in the vice.

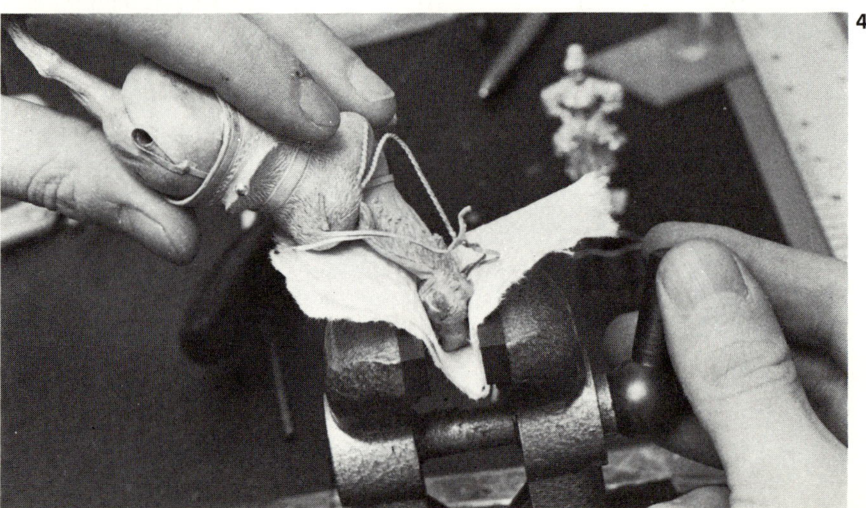

4

Opposite: This *chasseur à cheval de la Guarde* by Ray Lamb is, in my opinion, possibly the most outstanding 54mm figure ever produced from Historex parts. It is the culmination of the fine skills of animation, detailing, and painting, with which Lamb has earned an international reputation.

5 After roughening the edges of the cut surface with cross-hatching, fine-grained Polyfilla was applied. It is essential that all areas to be filled are solidly packed with filler so it was forced into all the crevices. The horse was then set aside to dry.

6 Next the head of the rider was severed at the base of the collar. After the slack of the sash had been removed, the torso was sawn from the legs, and the right arm was removed at the elbow. A cut was made under the right arm upwards towards the shoulder.

7 The limb was bent outwards and backwards. The right leg was put in the vice and carefully bent straight and twisted slightly outwards. The figure was then reassembled – all the parts being in the correct positions for the pose chosen.

5

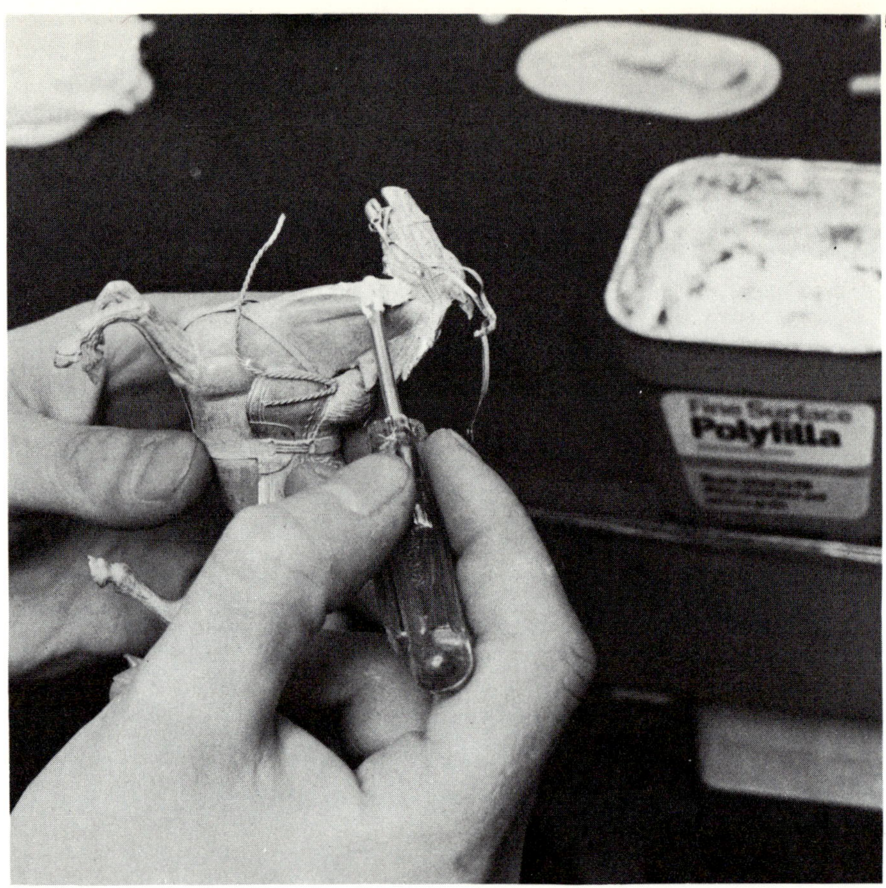

6

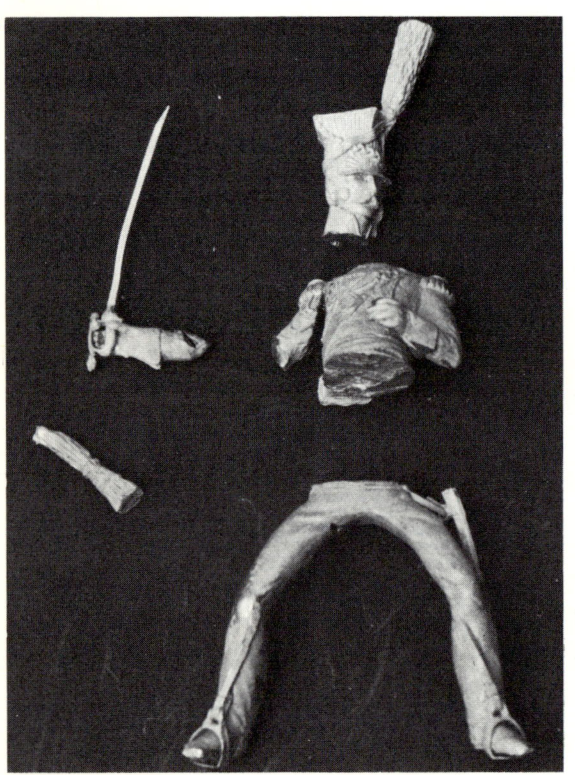

7

8

8 Filler was applied where appropriate and filed and sanded into shape when dry.

9 Reins, halter, and tail were rebonded to the horse. The horse was then bonded to the base and, because of the weight of the whole figure, a steel peg was inserted under one of the front legs for support. The figure was ready for priming and painting, as on the left.

9

Plastic

It must be obvious that the plastic medium provides greater scope for the animator and converter. The material is much easier to work with than metal and, if you ruin one piece of a kit, it is easily and cheaply replaced. Due to the greater variety of pieces in most plastic figure kits you have the added advantage of being able to mix bits and pieces from every manufacturer's products to arrive at any number of variations and conversions. The skills you develop are the only limitations to what you can eventually achieve. Witness the extraordinary scene of the consecration of John of Gaunt, created by the incredibly talented Ray Anderson using for the most part Historex figures, which are entirely Napoleonic. (See page 24.)

By far the greatest scope in animating and converting can be accomplished when working with the hard plastic medium, polystyrene. Unlike soft polythene, the use of which I advise only as a last resort, polystyrene has almost everything to recommend it to the modeller. It bonds rapidly to itself and with other mediums, it can be manipulated easily under heat, and with appropriate tools it can be carved, moulded, stretched, etc. It is the answer to the dedicated do-it-yourself converter's prayer. Conversions are being done today with polystyrene that would have defied imagination a few short years ago.

Opposite: **This scene of the consecration of John of Gaunt by the Archbishop of Canterbury is the work of Ray Anderson of California. He is undoubtedly the most outstanding artisan in the figure world today.**

Below: **This lovely military chess set by Edward Surén represents Napoleon's campaign in Egypt against the Mamelukes. There is a variety of scales within the set, the largest being the Kings and Queens at 60mm.**

1 Conversion can mean the creation of a figure unique to your own imagination. Ray Anderson's conversion of a Historex Napoleonic general officer into a barbarian Hun demonstrates the suitability of this plastic product for such work. The excellent detail in the original figure, the ease of modification, the lightness and ruggedness of the material, and, finally, the ease with which it can be painted without losing any of the detail, are all positive advantages. A special requirement for this conversion was a selection of 10-, 20-, and 30-mil sheet plastic.

1

2 Having detached the figure from its base, divide it into three pieces, cutting it at the waist and below the collar. Start by repositioning the ankles. Cut the feet off at the ankle and, using appropriately tapered wedges, cement them in the desired position. Repeat the same operation at the knees. Next make a cut from the waist down to the crotch, and, taking a flat 30-mil shim, glue it between the legs to widen the hips. Then the upper body is cut lengthwise front to back with the razor and widened with a 30-mil flat shim. The upper body is glued to the leg assembly, adding an appropriate wedge at the waist if the body is to be leaning forward. After the body-leg joint has hardened for twenty-four hours, make diagonal saw-cuts from the hip bone to the crotch, removing the legs. Using substantial wedges, reposition the legs in relation to the body and cement in place. Trim the collar from the neck and the ears from the head; for an open mouth, drill out surplus material saving the upper lip. After adding an appropriate wedge, glue the head to the body. The appearance will improve if a 30-mil shim is added to the neck. The arms are cut off at the shoulders and modified at the elbows with more wedges. When the arms are re-attached, again with wedges, the wrists are altered to suit.

2

3

3 After the figure has thoroughly dried, carve away the surplus material, including the wedge ends, sleeve ends, boots, etc. Any large cavities such as at the hip should be filled in with melted sprue using the Pyrogravure. Smaller cavities and the body structure are built up with body filler, the muscles, collar bones, rib cage, etc. being added as required. To ensure a hard, dense surface, apply several extremely thin layers of filler, letting each dry overnight. Filler in this instance is derived from a mixture of liquid polystyrene cement and sprue. Although clothing may be added later, the figure will be more realistic if the body structure is roughed in with filler first. Teeth can be glued into the mouth cavity. The lower lip is added by waiting a few minutes until a hard film develops on the filler and then pushing it up in front of the lower teeth. The ears are cut from 10-mil sheet and the details added later with filler.

4

4 The clothing details can be cut from cleansing tissue, adding the appropriate wrinkles. The tissue is covered with several coats of filler. Additional wrinkles can be added by laying on beads of filler and shaping them into realistic wrinkles after the skin has formed. A thick layer of filler can be used as a base for hair and fur. After drying, it can be textured with the Pyrogravure, using either a single fine point or the flat blade that has tiny teeth cut into its edge.

Mixed Mediums

With a bit of experience and with the materials available today, you can accomplish surprisingly successful results by mixing your mediums – polystyrene, polythene, metal, balsa wood, paper, or any other handy bits and pieces which will serve your purpose. A plastic head from here, the addition of belts and straps from there, removal of buttons and addition of others in appropriate places, changing or adding other equipment can completely alter a figure.

Before starting a conversion, you must consider your subject matter very carefully and select the elements you are going to combine with even greater care. If you make a bit of a mess of things at the start, do not be discouraged and above all do not throw anything away. Soon you will find that cannibalization of parts is the very foundation of successful animating and converting. By combining bits from inexpensive toy figures and military kits a superb miniature can be created. It only requires imagination, skill, and ingenuity, plus a good foundation of research. You don't have to spend a lot of money to end up with some excellent pieces in your collection.

Mr Roy Dilley, the President of the British Model Soldier Society, is one of the most adept converters of inexpensive model soldiers into highly imaginative and exquisite little works of art. I recommend strongly his book *Scale Model Soldiers* for he is a great advocate of mixing all mediums in his conversion work. He also advises the use of inexpensive models like Britains when working major metal conversions.

1

1 For his conversion Roy chose a Britains polythene military rider figure from the 'Horse Show' series (*right*) and converted it into a 10th British Hussar (*left*), such as was serving in Afghanistan in 1879. Out of his spare-parts box came the following items: a metal head and rifle in its scabbard from Rose miniatures; the polystyrene canteen, water bottle, knapsack, fodder bag, cartouche, and blanket roll from two Airfix kits, the Scots Grey and the British Hussar; and a polystyrene sword and bridle bit from Historex spare parts.

2

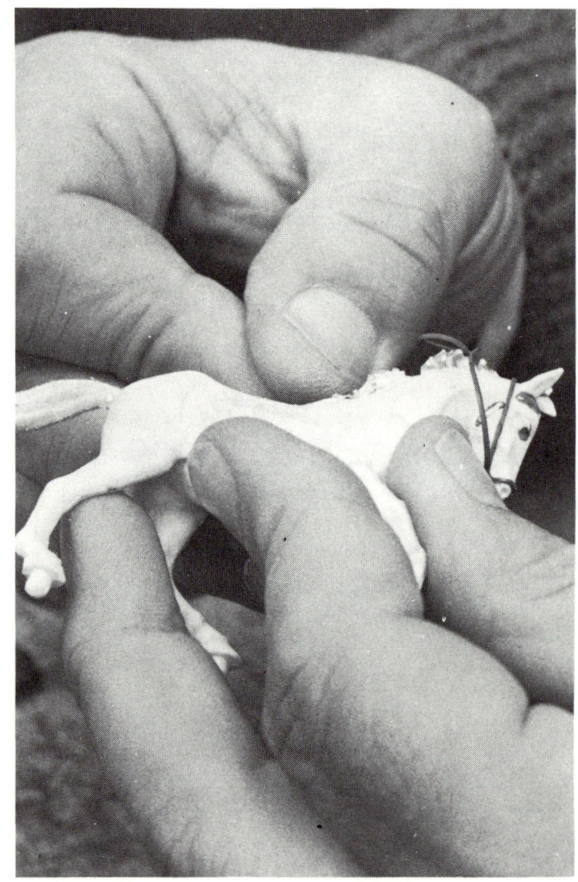

2 The first step was to take the rider from his plug in the back of the horse, cut off the soft plastic reins, and remove the saddle. Then, with a very sharp craft knife all flash lines were carefully shaved off the horse and figure. It is extremely important that the blade used is very sharp because this soft plastic shreds easily, leaving hair lines on the figure.

3

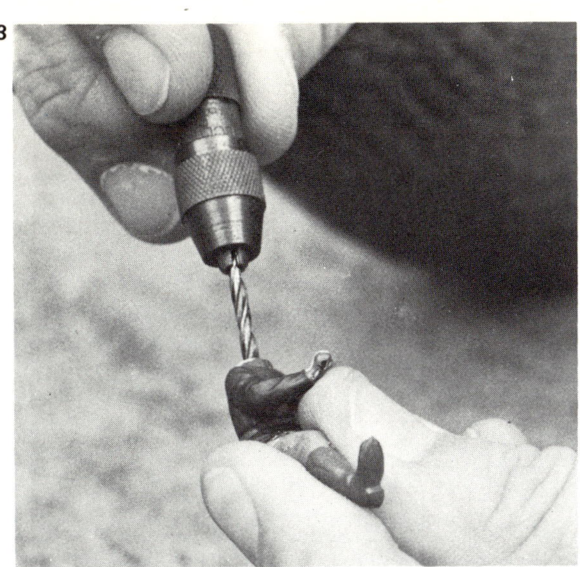

4

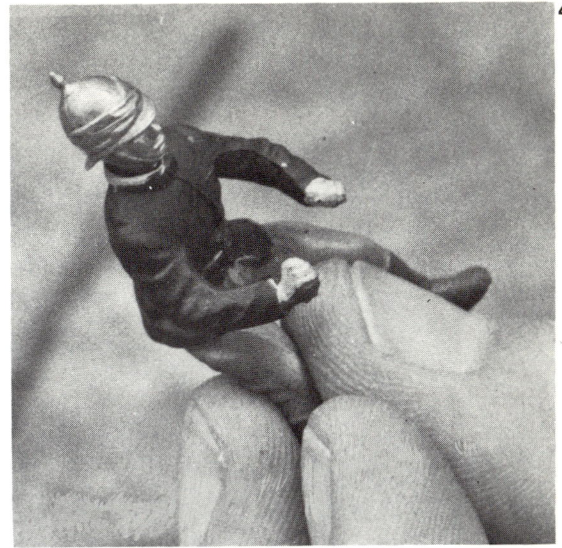

5

6

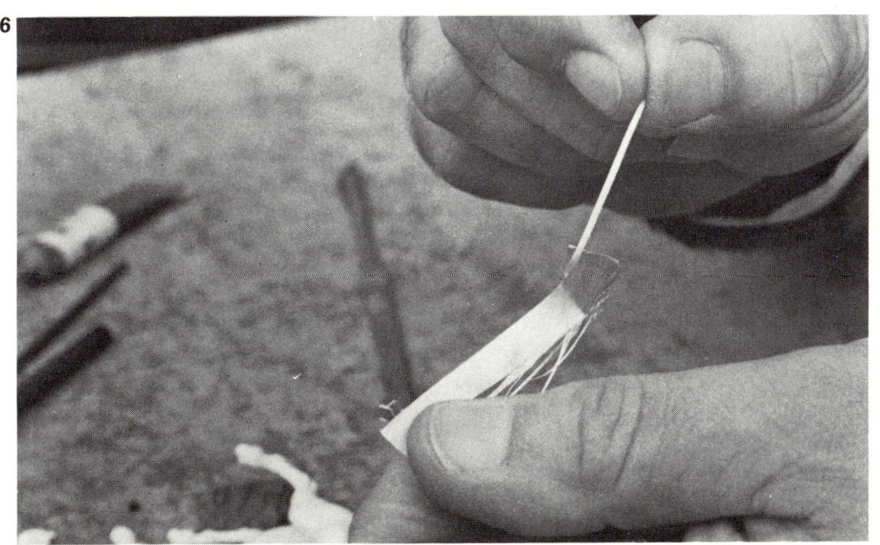

3 The head of the figure was then cut off and a hole drilled in the body to accept the new metal head.

4 The neck of the head should be roughened by cross-hatching to give the Devcon epoxy a better grip.

5 The boots on the figure were shaved down to resemble leggings, and small pins were driven into each shoe and cut off to represent spurs. All the holes and imperfections were then filled using Milliput filler.

6 Straps for the knapsack, water bottle, and cartouche pouch were cut to the appropriate length from self-adhesive gift-wrapping ribbon.

7 & 8 The equipment and appropriate straps were then bonded to the figure in the correct order. Humbrol PVC glue was used to bond to the PVC figure and Mekpac for bonding the polystyrene equipment together.

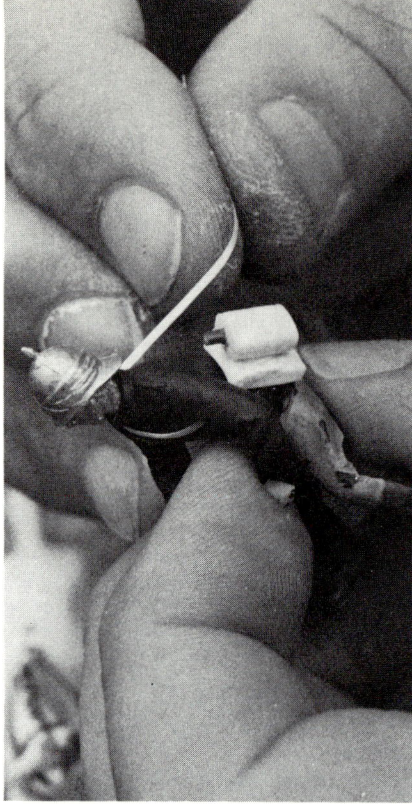

7

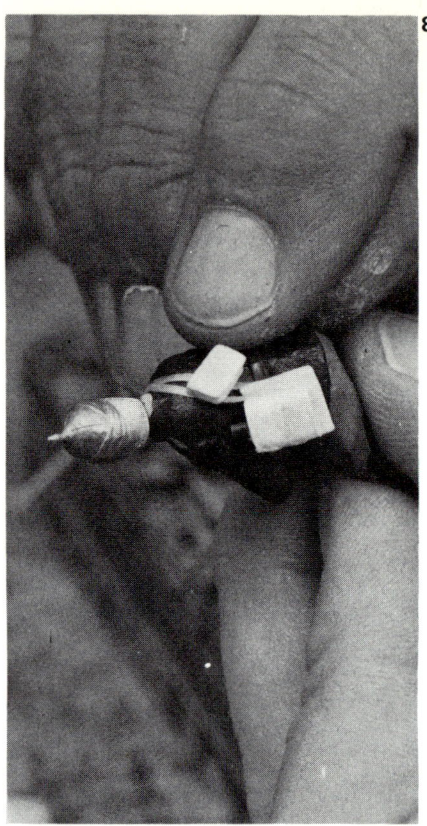

8

9 Stirrup leathers, also cut from the adhesive ribbon, were passed through stirrups from an Airfix kit and then glued to each leg. Shoulder straps from a Scots Grey kit were added and the rider was now complete.

10 A halter rope was fashioned from a piece of wire twisted to simulate the appropriate knots and anchored under the cheeks of the horse by pushing it into the polythene. Ribbon girth and reins were then cut and applied, using the Historex bit.

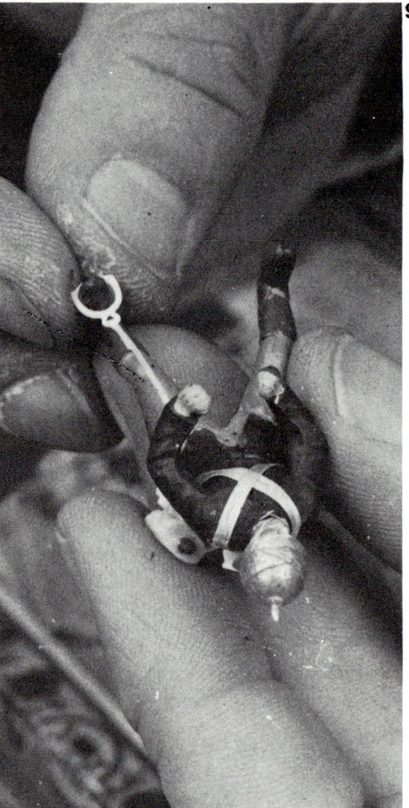

9

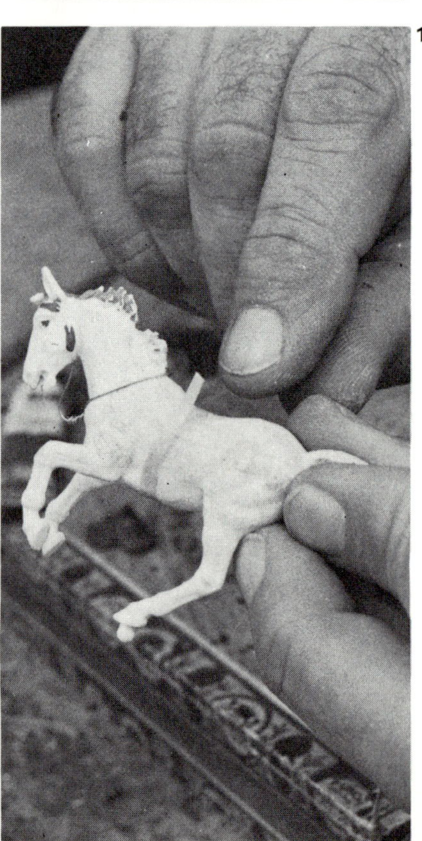

10

11

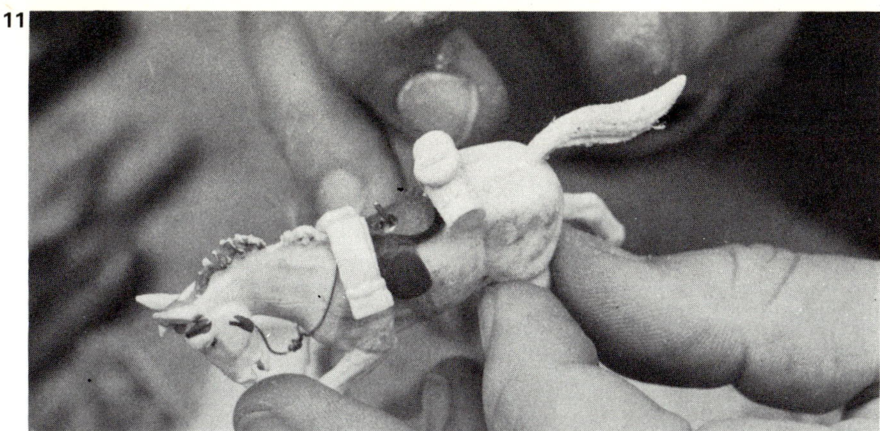

12

13

11 The original saddle from the Britain figure had the pistol holster removed and was then bonded to the horse with PVC glue. A pin was driven into the saddle of the horse. When the rider and horse were finally assembled, after painting, the figure was driven onto this pin to pose it properly on the mount. The Scots Grey blanket roll was shortened to the proper length and bonded on, followed by the Airfix haversack and fodder bag, and a mess tin converted from the Airfix water bottle.

12 The entire figure was then painted with Uni-Bond. This creates a solid skin and shrinks onto the figure. It acts both as a filler and a bonding strengthener.

13 The conversion was now ready for priming and painting. Roy was amazed to find that he was able to accomplish this job in a matter of a few hours after dinner one evening.

The animation of a plastic 54mm horse kit. First the three Airfix horses are made up according to kit instructions. Then, using only the three basic horses, Mac Kennaugh did the conversion shown in the second picture. The last picture demonstrates further possibilities which can be achieved by additional cutting and reassembling.

Opposite: These superb 12-inch dressed drummers are the work of Eugène Lelievrepre, artist to the French Army. Every detail of their costumes is made according to scaled patterns and with materials in the proper scale. They are truly exquisite miniature masterpieces.

5: Sculpting and Casting

Having tried assembling, animating, and converting, you may reach such a fever pitch of enthusiasm that you can be satisfied only by creating a figure of your own from beginning to end. Be warned that you are in for a lot of hard work and possibly a great deal of frustration in the attainment of your goal, but you will also be joining a rarified and very special group of military modellers.

It must be assumed that you possess some sculptural ability because it is not the purpose of this book to teach you how to sculpt military miniatures. Volumes have been written on the subject of sculpture. Our demonstration will begin from the point when you have created a figure from plasticine, or any other of the many suitable materials available today, and will serve to illustrate one method of casting your own figures.

This method will give you only a few master castings; it is not designed for any form of semi-massproduced figures. You may have many disappointments at first but as you gain experience you will triumph in the knowledge that you have created unique figures that are all your own work.

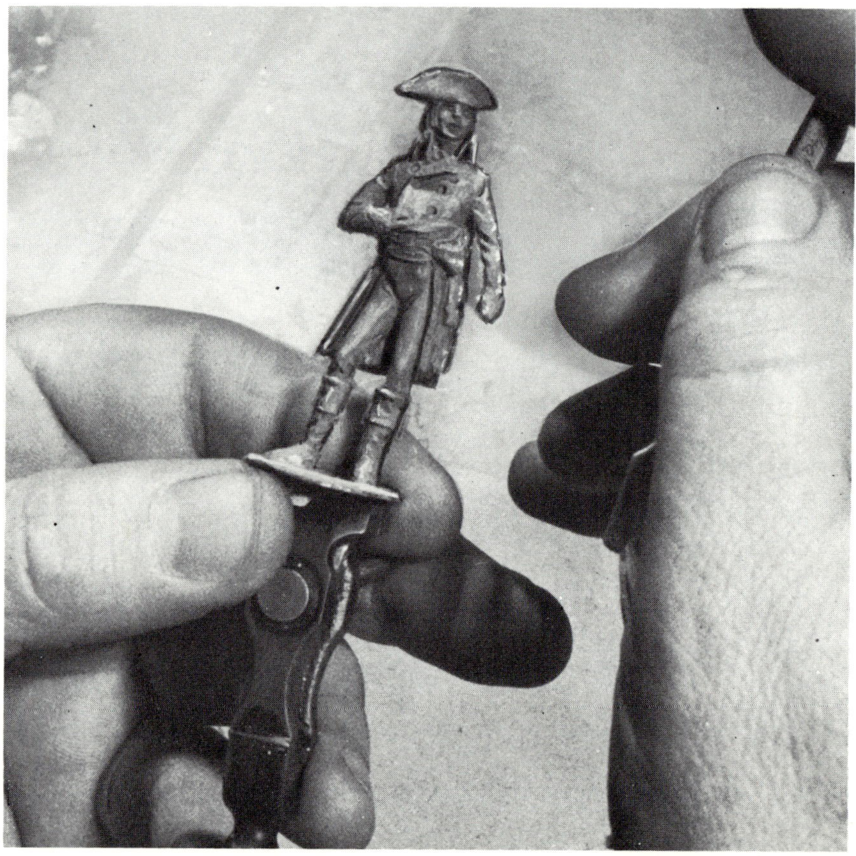

1 Edward Surén chose brown plasticine to create the figure illustrated. (This figure and two others were used to illustrate the rest of the sequence.)

2 

2 With plasticine of a different colour, he built a bed around one half of the figure. Three indentations were made in the plasticine bed – the keys which would lock the two parts of the mould together. The figure and the mask were then carefully brushed with powdered French chalk. Next he neatened the outer edges of the plasticine bed to make a rectangle.

3 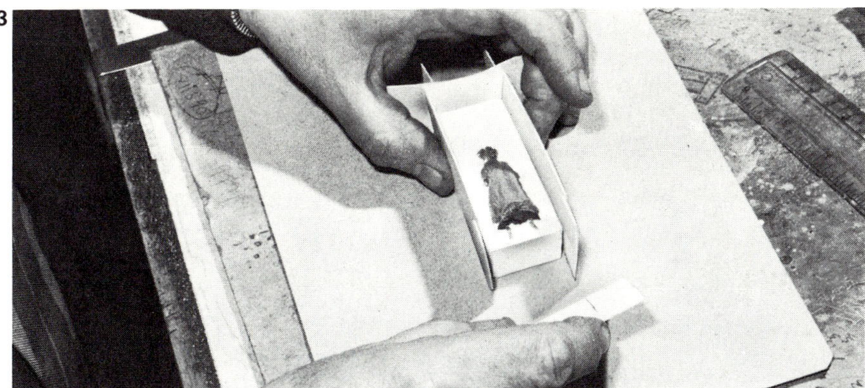

3 He made a cardboard mask which fitted around the bed and had at least twice its depth so that no part of the figure projected above the mask.

4 

4 He then mixed together measured quantities of Cold Cure Sylestimer, which is a rubber solution, and its catalyst. The resulting solution was poured over the figure and the whole thing was put to one side for at least twenty-four hours to give the rubber ample time to set.

5 When it had cured, he turned the mask over and very gently and carefully removed the plasticine bed. With this done, he was ready to make the second half of the mould, but before mixing and pouring the rubber Sylestimer he brushed more chalk around the inside of the mask and over the figure. After another twenty-four hours, he was able very gently and slowly to separate the two halves of the mould.

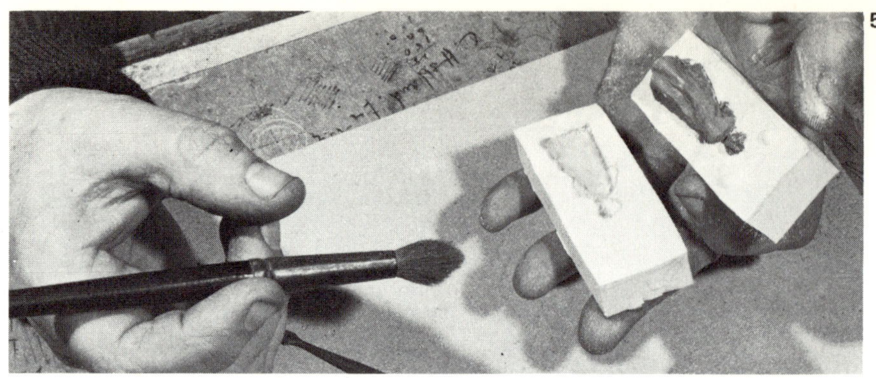
5

6 The plasticine master was removed with great care from the half in which it had remained. You may damage your plasticine master when you are removing it but do not worry as long as no plasticine remains in any part of the rubber mould. The next step was to cut a pouring channel into each half of the mould. When this was done he was ready to heat his metal to liquid form and pour it into the mould.

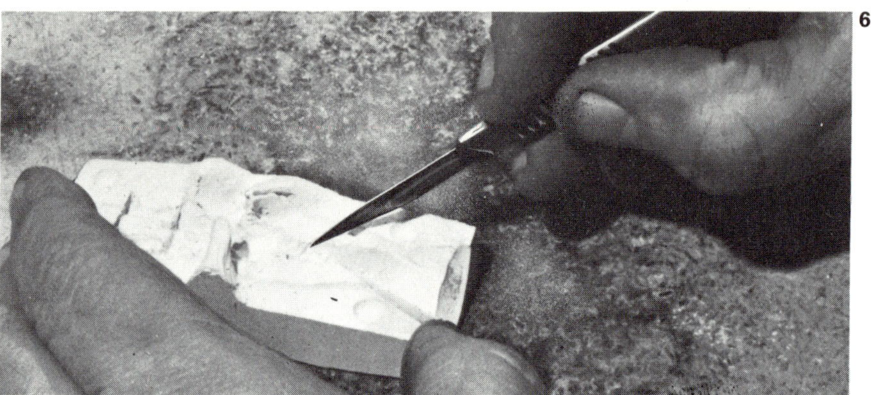
6

7 Edward Surén uses an alloy which is over ninety per cent tin. He can tell by the colour of the molten metal and its consistency when it is ready to be poured. Before pouring the metal, he skims its surface with the ladle because all the imperfections float to the top. He placed the two halves of the mould firmly together between two blocks of wood and, shielding that hand with a thickly folded cloth, he ladled the metal into the mould with the other. Needless to say, great care must be taken when pouring.

7

8 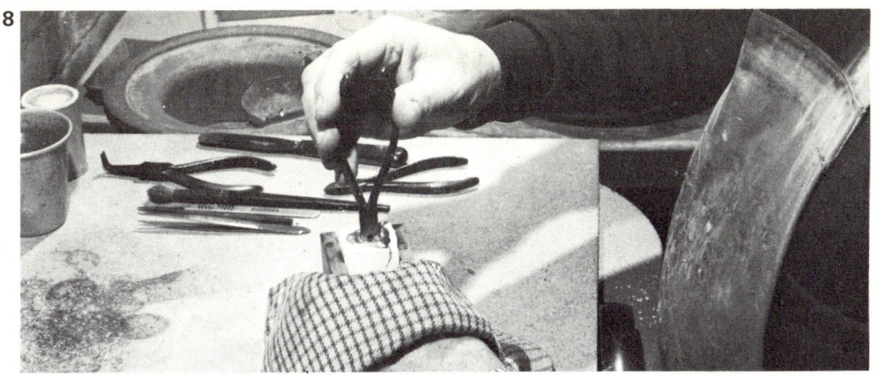

8 When the metal reached the upper mouth of the pouring channel, he banged the mould on the table to ensure that it flowed down into all parts of the mould. The unused metal was put back into the crucible.

9 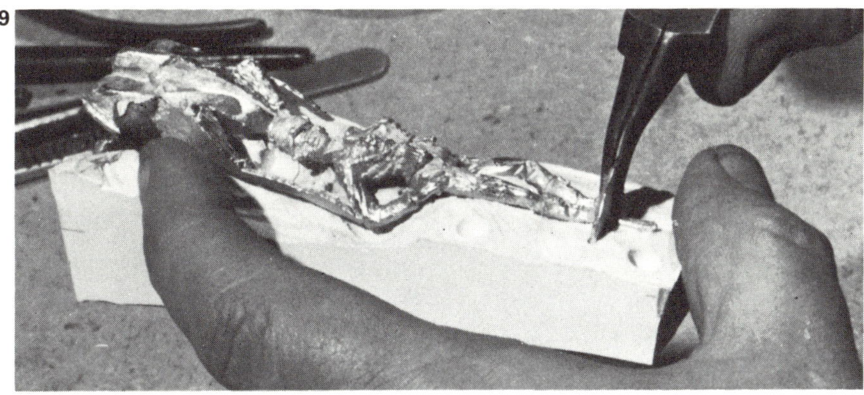

9 He let the mould cool for a few minutes before putting it down. It was cool enough to handle before he tried to separate the two halves and remove the casting. If you are lucky and the under-cuts on your figure are not too drastic, the rubber mould should last through about a dozen castings.

10 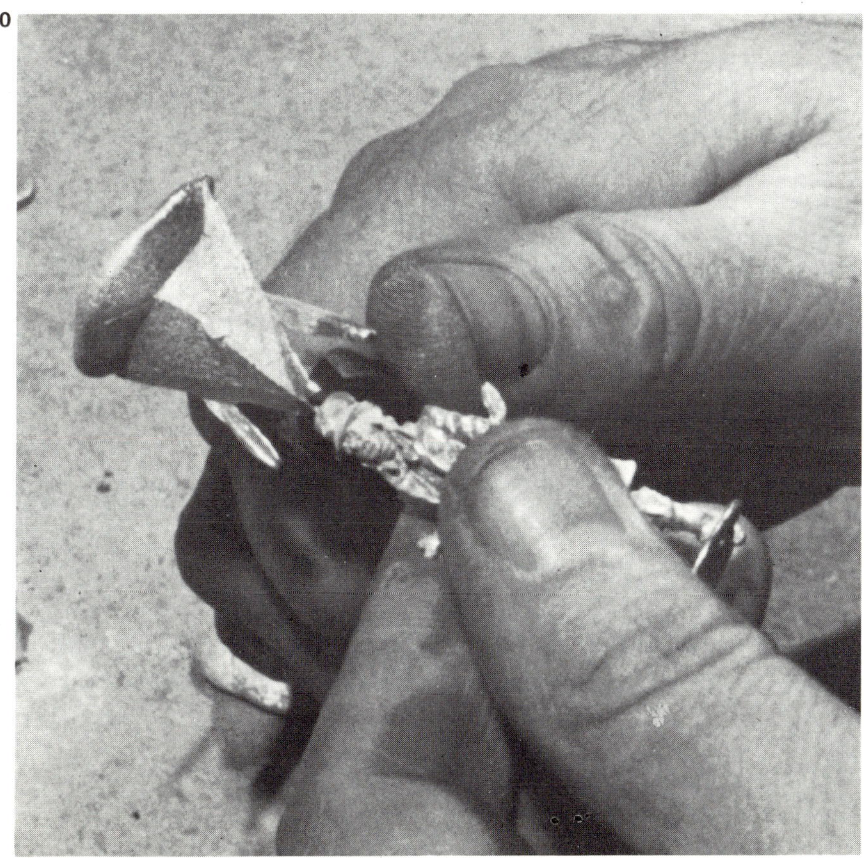

10 Lastly he pinched off the cone formed by the metal which had cooled in the pouring channel.

6: Painting

Every military miniature stands or falls on the quality of its painting. The finest castings, the most imaginative animations and conversions can be reduced to nothing by inferior painting. I have seen some brilliant animations at model competitions totally ruined by careless slapdash painting.

So, from the outset, you must spend a great deal of care and time when starting to paint a figure. With constant practice you will find your technique develops quite rapidly and you will discover which medium suits you best. Whether you choose poster oils, matt enamels, which are the basis of most paints produced specifically for modellers, acrylics, water-based paints, or artist oils – most of which we shall be examining in detail in this chapter – the care and patience you devote to painting your figures will reap their own rewards when you stand back and admire your finished work.

Again I must emphasize the need for patience and for taking things slowly at the beginning. One is always driven on by the desire to see a figure completed and to get at the next one, but for satisfactory results you must never rush your work at any stage and most particularly not when you are painting. You would be well advised not to leave other unpainted models in sight on your working table for they cause a distraction and may add to your impatience. Try to concentrate on finishing one figure completely before starting on another.

Equipment

As I mentioned before when discussing your arsenal of modelling equipment, be advised when acquiring your painting tools to buy only the best, particularly where brushes are concerned. A superior quality of sable brush may seem very expensive at the outset, but with proper care it will last you for many months or even years and you need only purchase one good set. Remember you are working on tiny areas and that inexpensive brushes have a tendency for individual bristles to stick out so that the heads never come to a proper point.

A good-quality Kolinsky sable brush will give you a superb point and will eliminate the necessity of having very small brushes such as Nos. 00 and 000. I know a number of outstanding painters who never touch a brush smaller than a No. 1 for even the tiniest detail. The better-quality brush not only gives you a finer point in larger sizes but it has the added advantage of retaining more paint per dipping and giving a smoother flow to the work. There is nothing more frustrating when working with a tiny brush than having it run out of paint at a crucial moment.

Care and storage of your brushes is very important. No matter what kind of paint you choose, it is vital that you clean your brushes most meticulously. Make sure that each time you use a brush during a painting session you clean it carefully in the appropriate thinner, remove as much of the pigment from the ferrule as possible, and put it down having reformed its point on a clean cloth. When you have finished your sitting, wash all your brushes using warm water and a mild soap, rinse them, and reform the points in the palm of your hand. Allow a little of the soap to remain in the brushes when you store them because this keeps the points formed, but remember to rinse it out before you use them again.

Brushes should be stored in a closed container. I use tall screw-top jars, but care must be taken to see that the brushes do not rest on the sides of the jar or you will find a permanent bend in the bristles the next time you wish to use them. I keep my Handover brushes on the cards on which they were purchased since these have two rows of elasticated retainers. This, however, is all personal preference.

The remaining tools, other than the paints

themselves, are extremely inexpensive. For palettes I prefer to use the polythene tops of coffee cans and throw them away after use. However all sorts of inexpensive paper palette blocks, small porcelain dishes, and metal mixing palettes are to be found in artists' supply stores.

I find a number of different sized screw-top glass jars have innumerable uses and can be had for no investment other than the consumption of their contents. If you are using more than one type of paint you must remember to mark each container of thinner carefully so that you do not mix them. It is also a good idea to use two or three different jars of thinner, one for cleaning the light colours, one for the dark colours, and one for metallics.

Paints and Primers

When it comes to the selection of paints, this will depend largely on your own personal preference, arrived at by experimenting and experience. Whether you choose to stick to one medium or mix several different ones is of little consequence. What really matters is for you to arrive at the technique which suits you best. In my own painting, which is of a very mediocre quality by present-day standards, I tend to mix oil-based poster oils with artist oils; as yet I have not experimented with acrylic or water-based paints. However, at the beginning of your painting career I urge you to stay with one type of paint until you develop sufficient proficiency to start experimenting in other directions.

There are several companies producing excellent sets of matt enamel oil-based paints especially for military modellers at very reasonable prices, among them Humbrol and Historex in Great Britain and Imrie-Riseley, Pactra, and Flowquil in the United States. In the water-based category, there are excellent paints produced by Rose and by Plaka, and Rowney has a high reputation in the acrylic field. Oil paints are discussed a little later on in this chapter, on page 42.

Remember never to use gloss paint on a miniature for it will instantly reduce it to the stature of a toy. The only area where gloss is viable is on such things as metal work or polished leather and even here careful shading is more appropriate than high gloss. Different textures can be achieved in all mediums.

When working with metal figures it is essential to undercoat the figures with a good primer because some metals react chemically with the paint and in time may cause corrosion much like that found on car batteries. The resultant tragedy – the deterioration of a fine miniature – can be avoided by the use of a good commercial metal primer. The finest I have found for this use is produced by Imrie-Riseley. It shrinks like a skin on the model and eliminates no detail whatsoever.

Matt Enamel Paints

For the beginner it is best to concentrate on matt enamel paints. They dry rapidly and have the added advantage of being produced in many of the required military uniform colours.

An absolute must before starting any painting is to make sure your paints are thoroughly mixed. This is particularly necessary with the small tinlets or bottles of Humbrol or Imrie-Riseley military colours. If you do not mix these paints thoroughly, the balance of the pigments, the binder, and the thinner will not be properly established, and you will find an unwanted gloss appearing on the figure.

It is also essential to keep the containers tightly closed when not in use and to make sure the covers do not get clogged with paint, otherwise they will not provide a proper seal and the contents will dry out. If you find a skin of dried paint on the surface of your tinlet, throw it away at once. These small containers are relatively inexpensive and once the contents have partially dried, they are useless – the paint under the dried skin cannot be mixed properly and if used will give a granular lumpy surface to your figure.

Now to begin painting. Metal figures, as we have seen, require a basic undercoating; polystyrene plastic figures do not. If you have used a metal primer, usually a mid-grey in colour, it is best to give the figure several thin washes of white before applying other colours.

Painting a face

It is best to start the painting of any figure with the face. In the end the face is what makes or breaks the figure. No end of excellent detail-work on a figure can be vitiated by a badly rendered face.

First make a natural flesh colour from a mixture of white, yellow ochre, brown, and red. Apply this base colour to the face area. Next add a slight touch of crimson and yellow ochre to the flesh colour and shade the eye sockets, the sides of the nose, the slight depression under the lower lip, under the chin, and around the hairline. Then add a touch of white to the flesh colour and highlight the ridge of the nose, the sides of the nostrils, the chin, and the cheek bones under the eyes. Add a little red to the flesh colour and touch in the cheeks and the lips. Now blend it all in with an almost dry brush. Add a slightly darker touch of crimson to the flesh colour to pick out the nostrils, ears, and a thin line between the lips.

Now, most important of all, turn to the eyes, which give the figure its character. First the white and then the iris and make sure no white shows under the iris. In actual fact very little white ever shows in the eyes, and it is important that you do not end up with a wide-eyed staring face. Add a thin darker line of shading all round the eyes and blend the lower lids to the bottom of the eyes. It may be a help when painting the top of the eyelid to turn the figure upside down so that you can paint the lines more evenly.

If you have difficulty in placing the irises in the dead centre of the eyeballs, try to make them look to one side or the other. The essential thing is to have them in identical positions. Eyes are certainly the most difficult part of successful figure painting but with practice you will soon develop your own technique.

Painting a figure

You are now ready to carry on with the rest of the figure. It is best to block in all your light areas first – that is your whites, buffs, and light colours – and paint in the dark colours last. Another word of caution here: try not to paint in small patchy strokes but rather lay a coat down in one even smooth stroke if you can, giving it a chance to dry before continuing. In this manner you will not roughen the surface of the paint by repeated strokes and the end product will give you a smooth matt finish.

When you have blocked in all your essential areas of colour, you are ready to bring life to your figure by adding shading. Examine all the folds and creases of the uniform carefully. Then mix a darker shade of the required colour and apply it to the depressions in each crease, blending it in smoothly. Now mix a lighter shade of the same colour and apply it to the crest of each crease, again blending it in very carefully. As your shading becomes subtler, you will find your uniforms acquiring a very much more life-like appearance.

It is best to leave until last all the metallic parts of the uniform. But remember you can shade metallic paints with appropriate colours, like brown for gold and black for silver, and finally you can highlight metallic parts with pure metal paint using an almost dry brush. By 'dry brushing' the high ridges of such things as cap badges, sabretaches, sword pommels, etc., you will add even more to the subtlety and realism of your painted figures. This basic technique of shading will apply, as you will see, to almost any type of paint – be it water-based, acrylic, matt enamel or artist oils. It will also apply to other aspects of miniature painting, including horses, scenery, and terrain.

Acrylic Paints

Acrylic polymer is a mixture of synthetic resin and emulsion. It is neither an oil nor water-based paint but a more versatile plastic emulsion with properties similar to both these mediums.

The only brand of acrylics recommended by Eddie Jones, an expert on these new plastic-based paints, is that manufactured by George Rowney & Company Limited. The three best suited for the model soldier painter are: Rowney Cryla, Rowney Flow Formula Cryla, and Rowney Acrylic Designers Gouache. It must be emphasized that these products are water soluble. They also cannot be painted directly on to plastic. Therefore you must undercoat, and, as acrylic paints dry waterproof, be sure to wash your brushes thoroughly.

Rowney Cryla is a very heavy medium and it is principally used for texturing and filling. It can replace the heated needle or Pyrogravure by the painting technique of 'peaking'. Peaking is done by dabbing a little paint on a surface and sharply lifting the brush away to leave a small peak of paint. Repeating this technique over an area representing a fur pelisse or sheepskin shabraque can produce very effective results. As texturing is the only basic use for Cryla, you only need one tube of white.

Rowney Flow Formula Cryla is the bridge between the oil texture of Cryla and the water-colour properties of Acrylic Gouache. It can be used directly from the tube as with oil paint, but it is thinned with water and not turpentine. It dries waterproof with a slight sheen in about a minute, and it comes in a range of thirty-six colours plus black and white.

Rowney Acrylic Designers Gouache has all the advantages of other quality gouache with the added benefit that it dries waterproof and to a completely matt finish in a very short time. It is opaque when used straight from the tube but can produce transparent washes when adequately watered down.

A further advantage in the use of Flow Formula Cryla and Acrylic Gouache is that different textures can be produced by combining them. For example, the cloth of a tunic is matt, whereas the texture of a face has a slight sheen, and hair and fur are never completely matt. By carefully mixing these two acrylics you can eliminate the use of varnish to attain gloss or semi-gloss effects. Flow Formula Cryla by itself will produce a not too-severe gloss, which is comparable to the sheen of oils. By adding varying quantities of matt Acrylic Gouache you can end up with a texture to suit every situation.

No single medium can solve every problem of figure painting but acrylics can match the colour range of any other medium and you can intermix them with any water-based paints.

A final reminder! Prime your polystyrene figures and clean your brushes quickly and thoroughly when using acrylics.

Oil Paints

Of all the various types of paint available to the miniature painter – acrylics, matt-drying enamels, even watercolour – oil painting, fully realized, is perhaps the most fulfilling. Admittedly, the techniques of application are somewhat difficult to master, yet, once some competence has been achieved, oils offer a degree of life, a blending of tones, a variety of textures, a vibrancy of colour, and a richness of subtleties difficult to duplicate in other mediums.

Miniaturists, in general, start painting with matt enamels. But, as a painter grows more proficient with enamels, it is not uncommon for him, or her, to decide to make an attempt at working in oils. Someone may have described the beauty of oil-painted miniatures or the painter may have seen a few examples done completely in oils, as, for example, those jewel-like figures by Mlle Desfontaine. Realizing that the same general principles of painting hold true no matter what the medium, the painter may plunge into oil painting.

Unfortunately, though the principles are the same, the technicalities are quite different. After painting two, maybe three, perhaps four figures, the usual procedure is to give up in frantic despair. To the painter's horror, the colours dry as glossy as glass, the surface shows every brush stroke, and the paint dries too slowly; it's with some relief that the painter returns to familiar matt enamels . . . thereby depriving himself or herself of a richness of achievement without ever knowing what went wrong.

Making a base coat

The first step in oil painting is to create a base on which to paint, a surface that will accept the paint cleanly as well as providing a foundation into which it can sink. As mentioned previously, a metal casting requires priming before painting in order to seal off the raw metal from the paint. Though enamels will take well on a primed casting, the primer surface is too slick for oils; the paint will slide on the smooth surface and streak. The greyish primer will also show through if the oil paint – especially lighter or transparent colours – is applied thinly, whereas a thick coat of paint will only clog detail, as well as showing brush strokes.

The answer is to give the primed casting a base coat of matt enamel. This can be either an approximation of the final colours or a simple coat of white paint. If white is used, it is best to apply it with an air brush or a spray can. Since white enamel is thin and semi-transparent, painting a primed casting would require a number of coats to cover the primer colour completely. Such covering is important if one is to paint on the white with light colours such as flesh tones, yellows, greens, or transparent reds. More often than not, several coats of paint-brushed white would clog the fineness of detail. Air brushing or spray painting provides a smooth, matt, opaque white surface in a few minutes with no loss of detail.

This base coat can be any matt paint convenient to use. Of the many different matt enamels with which I have experimented, it has been my experience that the American-made Imrie-Riseley colours provide a base most acceptable to oils. Other matt paints that I have tried seem, to me, to have a tendency to soak up too much linseed oil, causing the paint to 'drag'. However, I would suggest that you try different base paints until you find the one best suited to your work.

Choosing your brushes

The second problem the painter finds with oils is the selection of the proper brushes to use. Here, the technique of paint application becomes the determining factor. Matt enamels can be applied with almost any brush; the paint will usually flow into a homogenous coat, even if applied with the point of a brush. Oil paint, however, will not flow. It stays exactly as it is set down. Therefore, for larger areas such as pants and jackets, it is best *not* to use too small a brush or the point of a brush, both of which will only leave a residue of fine brush strokes. Instead, use a large brush – a No. 1, 2 or even 3 sable watercolour brush, depending on the area to be covered.

Do not limit the paint to just the point of the brush either. Instead, draw enough paint through the brush to fill the bottom half, then fan out the hair by smoothing and flattening the brush on the palette or even onto a paper towel. Fanning out the hair flattens the point and it is then possible to achieve a smooth and broad application of paint.

Oil-painting mediums

The number of oil-painting mediums is frequently confusing to the beginner in oils. Actually, there is only one with which you need concern yourself: a fine-bodied linseed oil. Shiva, Winsor & Newton, Grumbacher – any of these are suitable. Grumbacher also manufacture Oil Painting Medium I for use with oil colours where a matt finish is desired.

One frequent question is: 'Should the linseed oil be added to the paint?' This is generally not necessary as the paint itself has enough oil in it. The brush, however, should be dipped in oil from time to time – actually just the tip of the brush – to keep it moist while working. After dipping the brush into oil, wipe off the excess on a paper towel.

How to beat high gloss

One of the most discouraging aspects of painting miniatures in oil colours is the high gloss that usually results. A tunic that looks as if it was made of glass is, naturally, a depressing end to one's labours. Oil colours surface-dry first; the oil keeps slowly rising to the surface of the paint film, where it eventually oxidizes. However, this smooth skin of linseed oil reflects light as surely as a mirror; certain pigments – greens, dark blues, reds, and some yellows particularly – will reflect an enormous amount of light, giving the impression of a uniform made of high-gloss vinyl.

Obviously, the answer is to break up the slick surface, thereby diffusing the light that strikes it and so preventing the bouncing back of light reflections that give the impression of a high gloss. My solution is to mix a small quantity of Dorland's Wax Medium into the paint. The wax, a semi-fluid in form, will liquify as it is stirred into the paint. The wax-saturated paint will then have a textured surface of wax granules. This will break up and diffuse the light reflections on the paint surface, thereby eliminating the slickly-smooth surface of oil.

Wax granules on a painted surface, particularly on a figure less than three inches high, sounds like the very antithesis of the smooth surface the painter is working toward. However, bear in mind that we are here describing a surface in terms which require a microscope to verify them – the texture provided by the wax granules is absolutely invisible to the naked eye . . . it is even invisible under a powerful magnifying glass.

The quantity of wax to add to the paint is somewhat difficult to pin down precisely as it will vary from colour to colour. A very dark blue will require more wax than, say, a yellow or even a light blue. Too much wax will only serve to make the colour transparent. Practice and experimentation will soon provide a working knowledge of how much wax to add, but, roughly speaking, an average would be about one part wax to four or five parts paint, though darker colours may have to be about one third wax.

If the painted surface still shows a definite shine, even with wax mixed into the paint, bear in mind that this shine will eventually dry away as the oil rises to the surface and oxidizes. Though an oil-painted figure can be handled safely within about a week, it could easily take up to a year to dry completely. With time, as the figure dries, any shine will gradually tone down to an attractive faint sheen. However, as this could take months, if after about a week there is still a pronounced gloss, simply stir up a small quantity of wax into liquid form, then apply it with a large brush over the glistening areas. The wax is completely colourless and transparent; it will not alter the painted colour in the least, nor will it show any roughness, brush strokes, or granules.

Buying oil paints

As with brushes, buy the best oil paints you can afford. Since such small quantities of paint are used and since it does not dry out in the tube, an average-sized tube will easily last for years. Student oil colours, while inexpensive, are frequently not as permanent or trustworthy as the somewhat more costly paints. I have finally settled on Winsor & Newton paints for trueness of colour, fineness of pigment grinding, stability of binder, and permanence of colour. Shiva oil paints, slightly less expensive than Winsor & Newton, are also excellent.

Interestingly, manufacturers do not all interpret colours in the same way. Burnt umber, for instance – by Grumbacher, Shiva, Winsor & Newton and Permanent Pigments – is four completely different colours. There is an advantage to be taken of such differences, however. Permanent Pigments' burnt umber is a rich, warm brown, ideal for shading gold and warm reds; Grumbacher's burnt umber is a deep, blackish-brown, just the thing for painting dark horses.

Colour mixing

One of the extraordinary features of oil paint is the ease of colour mixing, producing shades far richer than those available in enamels. Cadmium yellow and ivory black, when mixed, produce a vibrant, intense green; Venetian red and ivory black, with a faint hint of white, will make a handsome brick red.

Grey is a colour frequently called for in painting miniature soldiers. Do not depend on a black and white mixture, which produces a perfectly neutral and flat grey: the range of greys that can be achieved with oils is seemingly limitless. A mixture of white, black, and yellow ochre will produce an unusually large range of greys; other variations can be mixed with:

white, umber, and Prussian blue
white, umber, and veridian green
white, Venetian red, and veridian green
white and umber

When painting white tunics, pants, leggings, and vests, remember that these were made of different fabrics. The slightest touch of ochre, blue, umber, green, etc. mixed with white will produce a variety of shades to indicate these differences. The end result will be more satisfactory than pure white, which has a way of taking on a chalky appearance when dry.

The newcomer to oil painting is often puzzled by the wide variety of colours available. The following descriptions will probably make colour choices (and colour mixing) a bit easier.

Ultramarine blue mixed with veridian green and white or Naples yellow renders delicate, atmospheric greens. With ochres, dull greens; with cadmium yellow or orange, vivid green. With umber and white, greys; with reds, violet; with alizarin crimson, deep crimson.

Cobalt blue has a similar scale with violet hues predominating.

Prussian blue produces greenish hues with all the warm colours; with yellow, an intense green. Mixed with yellow ochre, it will produce a dull green.

Veridian green, mixed with Venetian red, produces greys of extraordinarily rich hues. With Prussian blue and white, cold, silvery green; with cadmium yellows, vivid light greens.

Naples yellow is useful for lightening ochres, umbers, and burnt sienna. With black, it makes a neutral green; mixed with earth reds, it produces a warm pink.

Yellow ochre livens up the earth reds and umbers. Mixed with black, it yields a dull olive-greenish colour. It extinguishes the fiery hue of burnt sienna.

Cadmium yellow – both dark and light – gives life to ochres, earth reds, and umbers. With burnt sienna, it produces a fiery red; with black and white, a dull green.

Cadmium red can be used in similar combinations to the cadmium yellows. Rich and brilliant nuances are created when worked with yellows and blues.

Venetian red will give a fiery red when mixed with alizarin crimson, dull reds when mixed with black, and pink with white.

Alizarin crimson is highly transparent and, therefore, difficult to use by itself. It does produce rich warm tones when mixed with earth reds, vermillion, cadmium yellows, and oranges.

Burnt sienna livens umbers and warms the coldness of ivory black. With ochre, it produces beautiful vivid browns.

Burnt umber with black gives the darkest browns. With Venetian red, warm brown reds. As pure black has a tendency to dull colours, burnt umber is especially valuable for shading.

Ivory black, when mixed with alizarin crimson, creates a deep warm purple-black. Indian red will warm up ivory black. For colder tones, ivory black can be mixed with Prussian blue, cobalt, or ultramarine.

Skin colours pose a problem for the newcomer to oils; after all, matt enamels come conveniently mixed in a little jar or tin marked 'Flesh'.

Here, then, are some suggestions for skin tones. With white:

ochre, Venetian red, umber, and ultramarine
ochre, Venetian red, umber, and black
ochre, Venetian red, umber, and Prussian blue
ochre, burnt sienna, umber, and ultramarine
ochre, Indian red, and black
ochre, Indian red, and Prussian blue
ochre, Venetian red, and Prussian blue
ochre, umber, and ultramarine
ochre, vermillion, and burnt umber
ochre, rose madder, vermillion, and umber

Burnt or raw umber may be used, depending on the effect desired. The more red used, the warmer the skin tone; the more blue, the cooler. The umber neutralizes the blues to greys; the ochre gives life to these greys. Subtle toning can be added with vermillion.

Guard against making skin tones too pale. Soldiers of the past spent a great deal more time outdoors than do civilians of today and there is nothing like continual exposure to the elements for darkening the skin.

People often ask the question: 'What do you use to mix colours?' The quantities of paint squeezed from the tubes are small so the easiest things to mix paint on the palette, or to stir in wax, are toothpicks. Round toothpicks are best; they have more firmness and body than the flat ones and are less apt to snap while mixing a colour.

As for palettes, the best is probably the paper-pad palette available in art supply shops. When the top sheet is finally covered with paint, it is simply torn off, revealing the next sheet. This is certainly much easier than cleaning a wooden palette each time it is used.

One of the great advantages of working with oil paint is the smooth and unbroken blending that can be achieved. Most highlights can be accented by brushing in a bit of white (with the exception of reds, where white will create a cold pink). Infinitely subtle tones of highlights and shadows can be achieved with an absolute minimum of effort, due to the slow-drying nature of the medium.

Drying times

As for the slowness of drying, which often confuses and discourages the painter used to the rapidity with which enamels or acrylics dry, certain pigments will surface-dry much faster than others. Once you become familiar with which are the fast- and the slow-drying colours, it is possible to work on a figure for several successive evenings without waiting for complete drying.

As a general rule, darker colours have a tendency to dry faster than light ones. A dark-blue uniform, for example, can comfortably have its collar patches, piping, etc. added upon the following night without any fear of picking up the blue into the second colour. Reds, yellows, tans – most of these paler colours – will dry slowly. White is an especially slow-drying colour so try to paint white areas last or, if an entire uniform is white, set the figure aside after painting for about a week. In the meantime, while the white is drying, you can work on another figure.

If a figure is to be mounted on a white horse, paint the horse first and let it dry for a week or so, during which time the figure and horse furniture can be painted. At the end of that time, the horse should be dry enough to handle safely for the painting of the bridle, the glueing-on of the saddle, and other detailing. On the other hand, a dark-brown horse, primarily a mixture of burnt umber and burnt sienna, will be dry enough to handle the following evening.

These drying times are, of course, only approximations, intended only as a rough guide. External factors also enter into drying time: if the weather is dry and warm, paint will dry faster than if the weather is somewhat humid.

Under no circumstances should you attempt any artificial-drying short cuts, such as the application of heat or the addition of dryers to the paint. Artificially dried oil paint has a tendency to crack in time. One of your most beautifully painted figures could very easily develop an entire network of tiny cracks within a year or two – sometimes more. There is no guarantee that this will happen, of course, but it hardly seems worth taking the chance.

Texturing

Another advantage the painter should recognize is the thickness of oil pigment. Deft strokes of oil paint can create folds in sleeves and trouser legs or simulate the texture of fur and plumes. Once a painter becomes skilful at the utilization of oil paint to create folds and creases, the same principle can be used to add nostrils, lips, fingers – even finely textured moustaches and beards.

1

1 To illustrate the step-by-step method of painting a figure, Graham Bickerton chose to use Rose water-based paints mixed with Rowney Formula Flow Cryla acrylics. However, he tells me he is sorely tempted to paint horses with artist's oils. He emphasizes that all his basic techniques can be applied to any medium with only slight modification. The figure chosen was the new Ray Lamb 75mm line Grenadier officer as produced by Hinchcliffe Models. Graham strongly recommends that any figure, metal or plastic, should be undercoated with U-Spray matt paint, which comes in convenient spray cans and is a Borden Chemical Company product. (The medium is defined at the first mention of each colour and remains the same unless otherwise stated.)

2

3

2 A basic flesh colour was mixed using Formula Flow yellow ochre and transparent brown and Rose white, scarlet, and black. The entire area of the face and neck was painted with this mixture.

3 & 4 All the shading was then laid on with black.

5 A mixture of very light grey was painted onto the eyeballs, and then came a thin wash of transparent brown over the face and neck area.

4

5

6 Any colour can be selected for the irises, in this case Formula Flow blue, followed by black pupils.

7 The eyelid was high-lighted with light flesh colour. A wash of plain water was then used to blend the black shadow into the flesh.

6

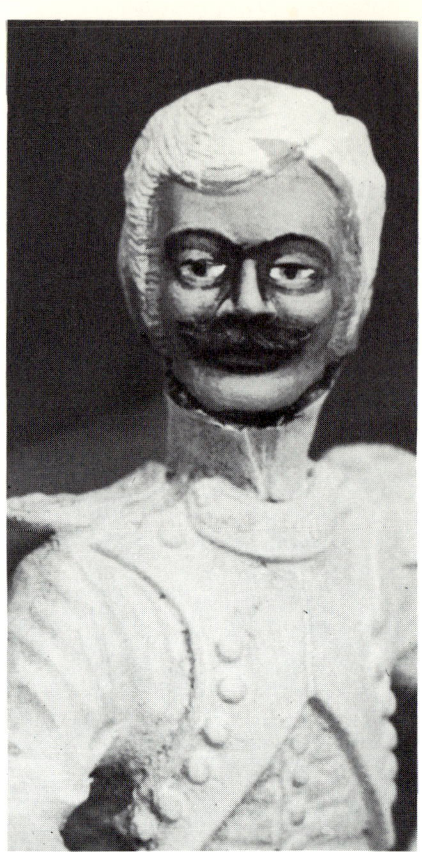

7

8 Light flesh highlights were applied to the upper cheekbones, under the eyes, on the bridge of the nose, on the nostrils, chin, and forehead over the eyes. The highlights were accentuated with a thin wash of black around these areas, blending the whole together.

9 The eyebrows and moustache were then painted on with a mixture of Rose brown and a touch of black. The lips came next, a mixture of scarlet, transparent brown, and flesh, lightened with white.

8

9

10 

10 Then the hair was put on with a base of Formula Flow black and dry-brushed with a mixture of grey and brown for highlights. Remember Formula Flow has a sheen to it and the degree of sheen is controlled by mixing with the Rose paints, which are very flat.

11 Next Graham Bickerton turned his attention to the uniform. First, the blue tunic area, including the epaulettes, was covered with a coat of black. Formula Flow black was then applied to the boots, bearskin, plumes, and cords. A mixture of scarlet and Formula Flow crimson – giving a true Napoleonic red – was painted onto the collar, the cuffs, and the crown of the bearskin. Formula Flow brown with a touch of ochre was applied to the turn-downs of the boots.

12 Next a mixture of Formula Flow and Rose dark blues was applied to the tunic.

11 

 12

13 The waistcoat and turn-backs of the tunic were painted white, and a touch of yellow ochre was added to the white for the breeches. The gorget was painted black. A thin wash of black was next applied to all shadow areas.

14 Highlights of thin white were touched to the breeches, lapels, and waistcoat, followed by light blue for the jacket.

13

14

15 & 16 Then all buttons, piping, seams, and metallic details were outlined in black. Rose antique gold and medium were mixed and dry-brushed on all metal parts, and on the bearskin, cords, epaulettes, and gorget. The sword, which had been painted separately in an appropriate gold, black, and white, was bonded to the figure. The plume was dry-brushed with scarlet, and the braiding and piping were painted, leaving the black undercoating to give outline definition. The hands were painted with a mixture of yellow ochre and transparent brown to portray soft kid gloves.

15

16

17 The terrain on the base was then painted with a coat of black, followed by dry-brushed coats of Rose dark green and light green. The rocks were painted with a mixture of blue, yellow ochre, and white, then dry-brushed with white. The rest of the base was given a coat of black gloss enamel, but that was purely a matter of personal choice.

17

Painting a horse

I am very partial to the painting of cavalry figures and derive the greatest pleasure from painting the horse itself. (It must be obvious that the horse, saddle, and rider should be painted separately whenever possible and assembled after painting.) I find artist oils are the most suitable medium for painting horses. However, I do give the horse a base coat of matt enamel in the colour I have selected before proceeding with oil colours.

Horses present such a wide spectrum of colour choices that I can only suggest you study as many colour pictures from books, calendars, posters, and postcards as you can before you start to paint a miniature horse. Being a horse lover, I have collected countless reference pictures and usually select a specific one to represent. Remember 'greys', as white horses are always called, are never really all white. They are subtle shades of grey, mixed sometimes with light tints of yellow, brown, or pink, and can be dappled with spots of strawberry colour. Greys present by far the greatest variety in markings – something you will discover with constant observation. A very white grey may have a pink nose as well as a black mane and tail; a very dark dappled grey may have a sparkling white mane and tail. Then there are palaminos, appaloosas, piebalds and skewbalds, buckskins, and roans, as well as the standard bays, chestnuts, and blacks – to say nothing of such markings as blazes, stars, snips, and strips on the faces or coronets, pasterns, fetlocks, socks and stockings on the legs – all of which must give you some idea of the myriad choices open to you in the painting of your cavalry figure.

However, remember, when choosing a colour, that military tradition favoured the mounting of units of cavalry on similarly coloured horses, although campaign exigencies often precluded this. Heavy units such as cuirassiers and dragoons favoured dark horses whereas lancers, chasseurs, and hussars preferred lighter colours and some Middle European hussars had palaminos and appaloosas. Trumpeters and musicians were usually mounted on greys, and kettle drummers on piebalds or skewbalds.

Again remember, when painting a horse, that the eyes are the most important part when it comes to giving it life and vitality. Very little white shows on a horse's eyes so put just a touch in the corners, the rest of the eye being filled usually with dark-brown shading into a black centre. The inner corner of the eye usually has a touch of pink, and the area immediately above the eye is a shade lighter than the all-over colour of the horse. You will normally find the areas around the nostrils and the lips are tinged with pink. All these are very broad generalities and serve only as a basic guide. For instance, I have seen horses with pink irises and blue pupils although weird-coloured eyes on horses are considered very unlucky by some people. The basic shading for horses should be done in much the same manner as for your foot figure.

* * *

Once you have started oil painting, I would recommend staying with it, no matter how difficult or unfamiliar it may seem at first. Do not be discouraged if your first few figures fall far short of what you anticipated. Nor should you worry about what might seem a costly waste of castings. Oils, like any paints, can be removed for repainting using a turpentine solvent. Great care must be exercised with plastic figures. Ordinary commercial paint removers can also be used with metal figures, but not with plastic.

Gradually, you'll find yourself becoming thoroughly familiar with the techniques of oil painting – learning by yourself what literally no one else can teach you. Once that happens, chances are no other paint will seem quite as satisfying.

You will soon discover that the most astoundingly fine details can be rendered smoothly and cleanly with oils; that the blending of colours, of highlight and shadow, will become so smooth that people may ask if you used an air brush; that the colours will not fade or dull down for years; and that oil-painted figures which have become dusty can be washed clean with no harm to the painted figure.

Once you learn the skills of fine detailing, there may well be no holding you back. In this respect, it is vital – for the creation of the most lifelike miniatures – that you learn to view the figure as a *whole*, not as a mass of meticulously rendered details. The surest sign of amateur art is too much detail compensating for too little life.

Top: **Marshal Murat and an aide de camp by Pierre Conrad, from Historex kits.**

Bottom left: **A second clever conversion by Mac Kennaugh, again based on Airfix kits.**

Bottom right: **Another example of Graham Bickerton's excellent work on a Series 77 hussar figure.**

FRENCH HUSSAR
REGIMENT
1794

Opposite top: Still the doyenne of military-miniature creators, Josaine Desfontaine demonstrates her incredible technique in this scene of Royalist ladies in the hands of Roundheads during the English Civil War. Scale: 60mm.

Left: A new star in the bespoke firmament, David Fordham created these magnificent 85mm seventeenth-century Persian lancers.

Bottom: The combined talents of Mâitre Eugène Lelievrepre and René Gillet of Historex produced this evocative diorama of the 7th French Hussars capturing the ice-bound Dutch fleet in the Texel on 20 January, 1795.

Here are two examples of the outstanding artistry of Pierre Conrad, an ex-trumpeter in the French Guarde Republicaine. His life as a cavalryman and his natural talent have made him one of the premier bespoke creators of cavalry figures in the world today.
Scale: 54mm.

Graham Bickerton again demonstrates his painting skill, this time with a Mameluke kettle-drummer (*left*), while Mac Kennaugh injects humour into his conversion skills in a scene entitled 'The Imperturbability of the British Soldier' (*below*), which demonstrates just what can be done with a basic Airfix horse.

Next spread: The action at La Haye Sainte during the Battle of Waterloo. A superb example of the fine work of Peter Gilder, creator of Hinchcliffe Model's 25mm wargame figures, in a setting of his own construction.

7: Dioramas and Scenery

The final step in the creation of successful military miniatures is their presentation. Whether it is a single foot figure, a small vignette of two or more related figures, or an entire battle diorama, the bases and terrain on which these figures stand are the crowning complement to all the work you have devoted to animation and painting.

A superbly painted figure without a proper base, standing on a carelessly painted bit of metal, looks unfinished and very amateur indeed. Put it on a small polished wooden base and surround it with an appropriate terrain and its value both visually and monetarily is at once doubled.

There are several companies merchandizing prepared bases of various sizes today, but a little ingenuity on your part can save you such an expense. Scenery and settings are almost as much fun to create as the figures themselves and I, for one, have always preferred my figures in vignettes which tell a little story or portray an incident. To me, this adds the final touch of realism to the perfection of a superbly painted miniature.

Whether it be large or very small, the same principles apply to any realistic setting used in the display of your figures. You must first decide how many figures your display will contain and what action or event you wish to portray. When making a diorama, it is very important that you preplan as meticulously as possible before starting the assembly. The contours of hills, roads, ditches, rivers, fords, fences, bridges, trees, etc., and the disposition of figures upon the terrain, should be carefully planned and sketched out on a drawing pad before you begin to think about assembling the various different materials you intend to use in the diorama.

One thing you must constantly bear in mind is that whatever groundwork you add to a figure it must remain in scale with that figure. It is also advisable to choose a base which enhances but does not overpower the figure or group of figures which will be placed upon it. When you have finished a diorama or scene it is a good idea to put it aside for a little while and then come back to inspect it objectively every few days until you are finally satisfied that it contains everything you had intended.

Certain materials crop up again and again in the creation of figure settings. Expanded polystyrene is a useful material in the making of hills. It is easily had for little or no cost from stores dealing in household appliances as it is now used almost universally for packing purposes. The material is strong, light, and easy to work with and saves all the drudgery that formerly went with the standard procedure of cutting terraced pieces of plywood and covering them with chicken wire before plastering. It is well worth mentioning at this point that the glue used on expanded polystyrene must be a carpenter's wood glue; Bordens Wood Glue is one such product. Other types will eat away the polystyrene.

Before the contours of the hills can be 'fleshed out', a hard covering must be laid down over the expanded polystyrene pieces. This is done with Modrock, a plaster-impregnated bandage netting which, when dipped in water, solidifies in about five minutes. It can easily be formed over the expanded polystyrene pieces to create a hard base on which to shape the terrain to the desired contours.

Polyfilla or plaster of Paris completes the task of contouring the terrain. It is essential that the plaster seals off all areas where such materials as liquid resins will be used because this prevents the resin seeping through any unfilled crevices and eating into the exposed expanded polystyrene.

Any clear resin product will do to create rivers, streams, and pools. The resin liquid must be very carefully mixed in the right proportions with its hardener, and it is also important not to exceed a depth of a quarter of an inch for each layer you apply. A layer takes about an hour and a half to set, and remember it sets from the bottom up to the surface. You can apply the second layer over the first when its surface is still a bit tacky. You can also create bubble effects and splashes just before the top layer sets hard. With a bit of practice there are all sorts of realistic effects which can be achieved with liquid resin.

One word of caution, however: you must keep your working area as free from dust or other airborne particles as possible when the resin is setting, otherwise your clear surface will be pitted. If any parts of figures are to be submerged in the resin, it is advisable to paint these areas with a waterproof paint; if you don't the resin may eat into the paint or even the underlying polystyrene if it is a plastic figure. Resin generates a lot of heat when it is curing so care must be exercised when using it with plastic. However, the spectacular effects that can be achieved in landscaping with clear resin are worth every bit of trouble you must exercise in its use.

Another material frequently used in the making of dioramas is a stone-plaster mixture which dentists employ in the casting of dentures. This catalyst powder sets hard in about five minutes when mixed with water, and is used to anchor trees and bushes as well as to create road effects, etc. You must remember that it generates a lot of heat when setting due to the catalyst action so again care must be exercised with plastic.

The selection of trees for dioramas presents a number of problems. Usually twigs or branches look terribly out of scale and those commercially produced for modelling purposes never seem to give the right effect. Nicholas Larkin, who takes us step by step through making a diorama on the next few pages, has found two solutions. Roots pulled from damp ground can make very effective bushes and trees, and so can selected branches clipped from juniper bushes and immediately sprayed with a heavy coating of ladies' hair lacquer. This spraying not only seals the branches but seems to preserve the colour indefinitely.

One last word of caution: creating a diorama of any appreciable size is a messy business, involving a number of mixing processes. Make sure you select a working area where sawdust, bits of plaster, drops of resin, and splashes of paint are not going to cause a divorce in the family.

1

1 Nicholas Larkin chose for his diorama seven Imrie-Riseley hussars painted in the colours of the élite company of the 5th Hussars of Napoleon's Army. As the figures were assembled in very animated poses, we decided to portray them in the return from a charge. A thin plywood base, measuring two feet by three feet, was selected since this gave us adequate room to contain an example of most types of terrain. Nick marked out the approximate position of each element in the terrain by drawing it in on the base.

2

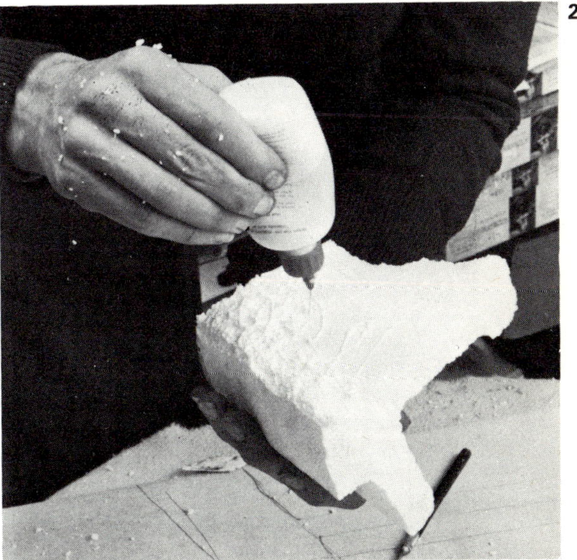

2 Next came the creation of the hills and depressions. For these, broken pieces of expanded polystyrene foam were glued to the base in an approximation of the desired shape of the terrain.

3 The ditch next to the road was then formed from strips of expanded polystyrene insulating tiles. All the basic pieces were now glued and ready to be covered.

3

4 Lengths of Modrock were cut to fit over the broken pieces of expanded polystyrene.

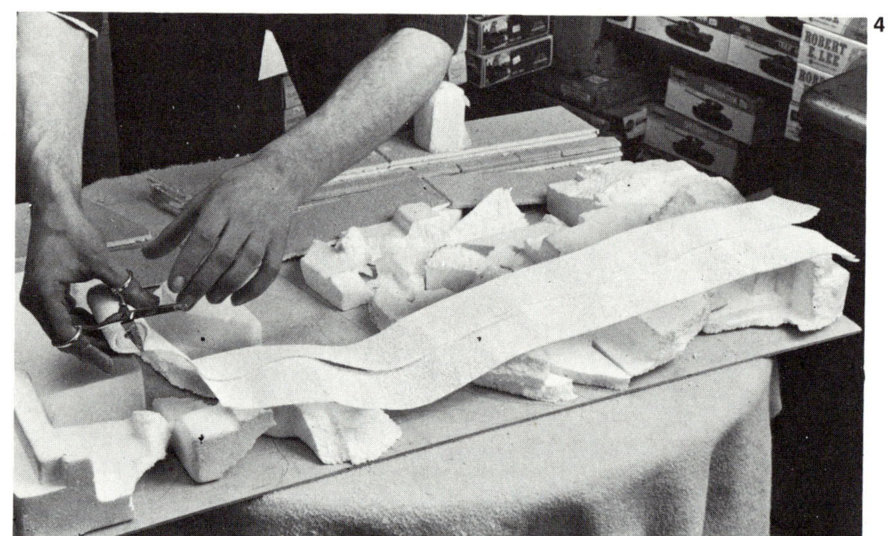

4

5 Each piece of netting was then passed through water to moisten the plaster . . .

5

6

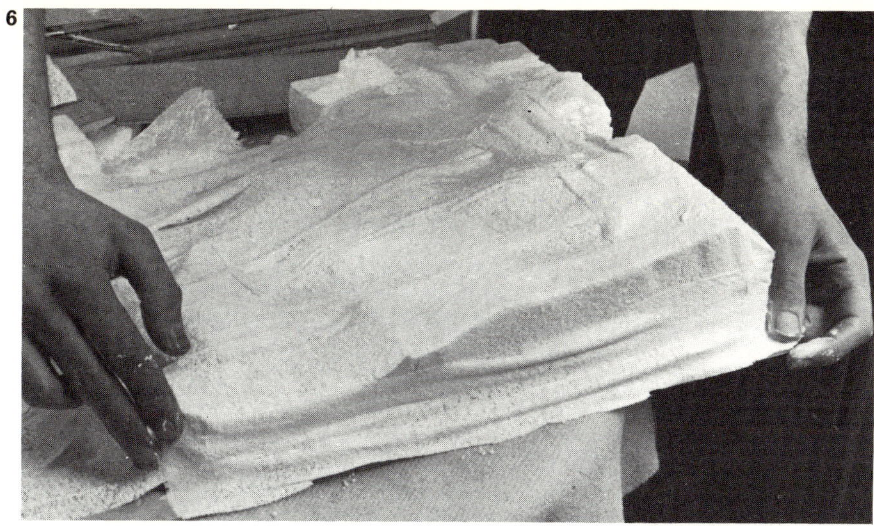

6 . . . and laid in position. The dampened Modrock dries hard in five minutes so Nick had to work quickly and smoothly.

7

7 Next several thin coats of plaster were applied to fill and shape the terrain to the desired contours. Special care was taken to seal off the bed of the ditch and the river so that liquid resin would not leak through and eat into the polystyrene.

8

8 Once the plaster had set, it was time to add texture to the terrain. The river bed and banks and the bottom of the ditch were now landscaped with an assortment of rocks, sifted gravel acquired from car parks and other sources, and plastic dust from a local moulding firm.

9 To achieve the effect of grass, all the desired areas were painted with a coat of polyurethane matt varnish . . .

9

10 . . . over which was sprinkled a thin coating of finely sifted sawdust. The sawdust should come from a cabinet-maker's workshop for this type is much finer than that available from lumberyards. It is actually sanding dust and renders the proper scale of texture for the ground.

10

11 We selected our trees and bushes next and anchored them in position with a stone-plaster mixture. The dead tree being secured here is a dead azalea plant, plucked from the garden, roots and all. It was set into the wet stone-plaster with some of the roots protruding, which gave it a very natural look. Elsewhere juniper bush clippings were planted to represent growing trees.

11

12

12 Then Nick was ready to begin adding the water effects to the diorama, using Isopon clear resin. Having carefully mixed the liquid, he laid several layers down in the ditch and over the river bed.

13

13 While the resin was still fluid, he positioned the galloping trumpeter in the middle of the ford. The figure had been removed from its base and the horse's legs painted with waterproof paint to prevent the liquid resin from eating into the oil paints beneath.

14

14 Very thin washes of oil colours were mixed and applied to the grassy areas, starting with shadow areas.

15 Next gravel was mixed into a portion of stone plaster and the road was created section by section. Figures were anchored in appropriate positions as he worked along its length. This stone plaster dries as hard as cement and it was not necessary to retain the bases of all the metal figures because they were set into it. While the mixture was still wet, he imprinted wheel ruts and hoof prints to add to the realism of the groundwork.

15

16 Finally, the whole terrain was set into a picture-frame base to give it its finished appearance. Despite its size, the whole diorama was very light – due mostly to the use of expanded polystyrene.

16

Here and opposite: Details of the completed diorama which give some idea of the innumerable possibilities open to you in the creation of lifelike settings for military miniatures.

In each of the following vignettes we see how a figure or two in a setting can tell a story. There's little doubt about the action in this scene by Nick Larkin.

A *landsknecht* at a fountain, by David Fordham.

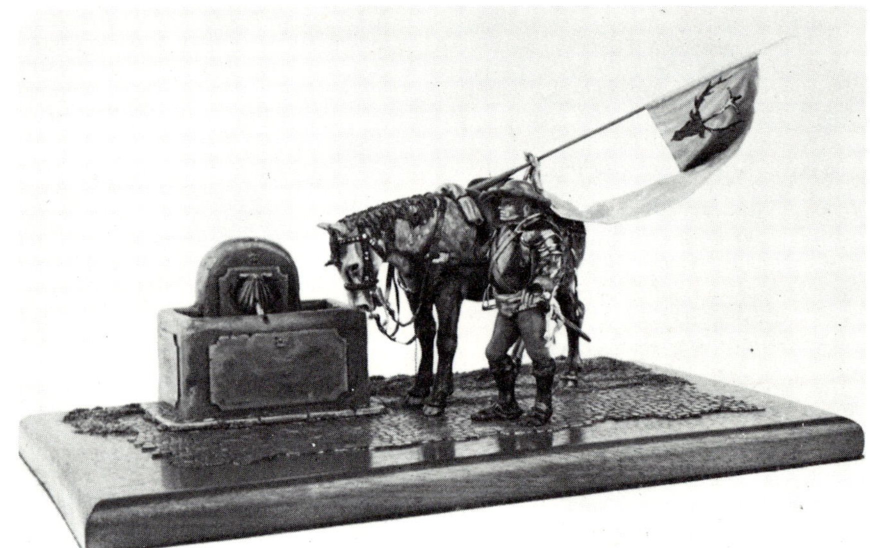

This scene might be titled, 'Do find my horse!'

One of the few solaces in a soldier's life.

A splendid 88mm German gun in its emplacement.

All the bitter cold of winter warfare is present in this episode by Nick Larkin.

8: Care and Display

When you have spent a great deal of time and effort to produce a miniature of your own, you will certainly wish to keep and preserve your treasure in the best possible condition.

Dust and heat are your two main enemies. If you keep your figures on open shelves, periodic dusting with a soft brush is essential. Even if you have glass display cases, they are not hermetically sealed and they and their contents should be dusted occasionally. If you have internal lighting in display cabinets, it is not a good idea to leave it on for long periods of time as the heat will build up inside and certain paints and metals may react to violent atmospheric changes. It will also be obvious that any display area should be as far removed from radiators and fireplaces as possible.

If you are making your own display cabinets, do not paint the interiors with anything other than water-based paints and make sure that the display case is thoroughly dry before placing any figures in it. This is especially true when any varnish is involved.

No matter what medium has been used in painting your figure, never at any cost pick it up by anything other than the base. (Here again is another factor which stresses the necessity of having adequate bases on your figures.) Fingers touching the figure itself will transfer an oily deposit which it is impossible to remove. You can be excused extreme rudeness to the uninitiated person who tries to pick up one of your figures with his fingers.

Methods of displaying your collection can be as varied as your imagination permits. For a long time I have searched antique markets for Victorian glass bell-jars. Today they are becoming almost prohibitive in cost but occasionally you may find one at a reasonable price, usually containing some moth-eaten stuffed bird or atrocious Victorian doll. Having expunged the contents and lined the bottom with coloured velvet, you have a dust-free means of displaying a few of your figures in a most attractive manner. I have also found old-fashioned brass kerosene lamps can be turned into attractive display cases by the removal of the lamp's innards.

With the present upsurge of interest in military modelling, several firms are making plastic domes and bases to accept one or more figures. It is also possible to have perspex covers made specially to fit over your small scenes or dioramas.

Another excellent way of displaying miniatures is in a self-contained shadow box with its own integral lighting system. Many modern interior decoration schemes are based on a modular system of wall cabinets, cupboards, book shelves, and other built-in furniture. I have found some of these units to be ideal for displaying parts of my collection.

John Ruddle has chosen a unique way to display his collection – by building whole armies in miniature cities in his garden. This, of course, is not everyone's cup of tea, but it certainly shows an immense amount of imaginative ingenuity.

Depending on the size of your collection there are countless ways of incorporating it into the decorative scheme of your home. As with all other aspects of this consuming hobby, the only limits are those imposed by your own taste and imagination.

Top: **Found on the junk heap of a church being demolished, this section of a choir stall stripped of its dark stain has made a very appealing wall display for some of my larger dressed figures.**

Bottom left: **Built-in wall cabinets with interior lighting make excellent settings for military miniatures.**

Bottom right: **This glass-fronted cabinet is just one of the many storage possibilities available if you use modular wall units as part of your decor.**

This antique brass wall light with its working parts removed makes an attractive display case for models.

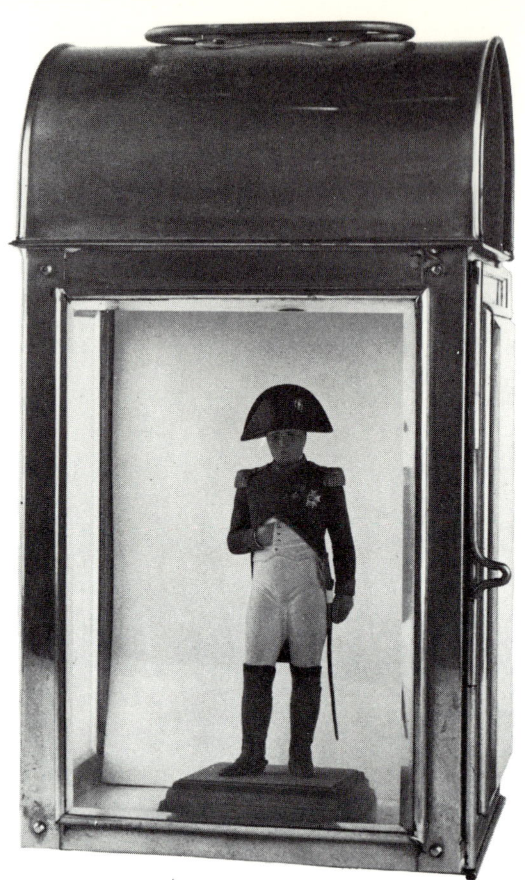

These Victorian bell jars are excellent decorative dust-proof display cases for single miniatures or small groups of figures.

Left: Occasionally one can locate a local cabinet maker who is willing to make small wood and glass cases such as this one. The great advantage is, of course, that he can tailor a case to suit a specific requirement, but this is not inexpensive.

Below: Certainly one of the most attractive ways of displaying figures is John Ruddle's miniature outdoor cities, inhabited by model armies winter and summer. He admits that the soldiers require repainting every five years or so, but then he has indoor armies as well, being a Britains collector on the grand scale.

9: Research

Once you have become a confirmed military miniature modeller, you will find that second in importance only to the development of your modelling technique is the research you devote to the perfecting of your figures. Indeed, a large proportion of the pleasure you derive from your modelling will emanate from the precision of your research. There is absolutely no value whatsoever in a miniature – no matter what the excellence of its painting and animation – if any of the uniform details are inaccurate.

Most kits on the market contain either a colouring guide or a coloured illustration but it behoves you not to rely entirely on these instructions for they are, at best, very rudimentary. You would be well advised to seek out other references and crosscheck them very carefully before embarking on any elaborate work on your model.

In a work of this scope, it is impossible to enumerate the countless resources available to you for your research so I will try only to point you in a few directions which may be of help.

No matter what period of military history you choose, there are an ample number of books, uniform plates, and in most cases museums which cater to that interest. Research by its very nature is time consuming, and it can be expensive if you choose to acquire your own books and plates. But every hour and every penny you devote to it will reap its own rewards many times over. Most good libraries contain the books you need and especially the libraries in military museums.

There are a number of outstanding military museums in the United Kingdom, Europe, and North America. Not only are their libraries available to you, but many of them sell books, plates, postcards, and other illustrations at very reasonable prices. Many British regiments have their own museums, and these have a fund of information, uniforms, and equipment for your inspection. Portrait galleries and art museums contain many military paintings which can be of great assistance when portraying specific people or scenes.

There are also a host of modelling and historical societies throughout the world. Most publish bulletins or magazines which are filled with invaluable information and most of them exchange their bulletins with each other. I urge any keen modeller to join one or more of these societies for the cost of membership is minimal in comparison with the benefits derived not only from the information and inspiration in their publications, but from association with their erudite and talented members.

Commercial magazines devoted entirely to military modelling are mushrooming in every country, and they also constitute a wealth of relevant research and excellent articles on modelling methods.

These suggestions are but a few of the more obvious directions for you to explore in the pursuit of accuracy in your modelling. I am certain that time and effort will offer many more. I would just like to recommend two which will be of further help.

The first is to keep a pictorial file of every cutting from newspapers, magazines, calendars, displays, brochures, and any other source that comes to hand which may prove relative to your interest. You will soon find you are accumulating a most valuable reference library.

The second suggestion is to keep by you a notebook in which you tabulate and, if possible, sketch details of uniforms and equipment wherever you go. Whether you are in a museum or watching a display, a military tattoo, or a parade, you can note down pertinent matters to which you can refer at a later date. Do not concern yourself with the quality of your sketching as long as you can interpret the drawings yourself. If you have any photographic ability so much the better. Either way, you will be accumulating a fund of valuable research material and enlarging your own knowledge of things military by leaps and bounds.

There follow two lists: one of relevant museums and the other of military modelling and historical societies. However, I must stress that both are very limited indeed due to our space restrictions. For a more detailed listing of international military museums I recommend Donald Featherstone's book *Handbook for Model Soldier Collectors.*

Museums

Austria

The Danube Museum, Petronell
Military Academy, Vienna-Newstadt

Canada

Canadian War Museum, Ottawa
Montreal Military Museum
St Helena Island Museum, Lake St Louis, Montreal

France

Brunnan Collection, Château de l'Emperie, Salon-en-Provence
Inter-Allied Museum, Arromanches, Normandy
Miniature Figurine Museum, Hôtel de Ville, Compiègne
Musée Carnavalet, Paris
Musée de l'Armée, Paris
Musée de la Marine, Paris
Strasbourg Historical Museum

Germany

Bayerisches Museum, Munich
Hersbruck Museum, near Nuremburg
Plassenburg Castle, Kulmbach

Great Britain

Battle and District Historical Society Museum, Battle, Sussex
Castle Museum, York
Imperial War Museum, London
Killicrankie Museum, Perthshire
National Army Museum, London
Public Museum and Art Gallery, Hastings, Sussex
Royal Armoured Corps Tank Museum, Bovington Camp, Dorset
Sandhurst Museum, Camberley, Surrey
Scottish United Services Museum, Edinburgh Castle
Tower of London Armouries, London
Woburn Abbey, Bedfordshire

United States of America

The Aberdeen Proving Ground Museum, Aberdeen, Maryland
Albany Museum, New York
Atlanta Museum, Georgia
The Custer Museum, Little Big Horn, Oklahoma
Fort Scaranworth Museum, Kansas
Gettysburg Museum, Pennsylvania
Monticello Museum, Virginia
Museum of the Cincinnati, Washington D.C.
Museum of the City of New York
Smithsonian Institute, Washington D.C.
West Point Museum, New York
Yorktown Museum, Virginia

Military Modelling and Historical Societies

Australia

The Military Historical Society of Australia,
20 Thomasina Street, Bentleigh East, Victoria 3165, N.S.W.
Secretary: B.J. Videon
Magazine: *Sabretache*

Austria

Gesellschaft der Freunde und Sammler Kulturhistorischer Figuren,
24 Hernalserhauptstrasse, Wien XVII, Austria.
Secretary: Dr Erich Kroner
Magazine: *1683*

Belgium

Société Belge d'Etude de l'Uniforme et du Costume,
365 Avenue du Kouter, Bruxelles 5, Belgium.
Secretary: M. Steodinck
Magazine: *La Figurine*

Canada

Miniature Armoured Fighting Vehicles Association,
R.R. No. 2, Preston, Ontario, Canada.
Secretary: G. Bradford
Magazine: *Tankette*

Ontario Model Soldier Society,
1 North Glen Avenue, Islington, Ontario.
Secretary: W. Peters
Magazine: *Courier*

Denmark

Danish Model Soldier and Uniform Society,
Broderskabsveg 15, Copenhagen F, Denmark.
Secretary: Paul W. Liebe
Magazine: *Chakloten*

France

Société des Collectionneurs de Figurines Historiques,
38 Rue de Lubeck, Paris 16e, France.
Secretary: M. Philippot
Magazine: *Le Bulletin*

Germany

Deutsche Gesellschaft der Freunde und Sammler Kulturhistorischer Zinnfiguren,
3167 Burgdorf Hann, Wallegartenstrasse 26, West Germany.
Secretary: Friedrich Schirmer
Magazine: *Die Zinnfigur*

Great Britain

British Model Soldier Society,
22 Priory Gardens, Hampton, Middlesex.
Secretary: J.T. Ruddle
Magazine: *Bulletin*

International Plastic Modellers' Society,
180/5 Cockhill Lane, Rubery, Birmingham B45 9SJ.
Secretary: Gordon Griffiths
Magazine: *Journal*

International Society of Military Collectors,
Belmont-Maitland Publishers Limited, 188 Piccadilly, London W1V 9DA.
Secretary: Lt.-Col. J.B.R. Nicholson
Magazine: *Tradition*

Irish Model Soldier Society,
61 Brighton Row, Rathgar, Dublin 6, Eire.
Secretary: S. Wade

Military Historical Society,
7 East Woodside, Leighlands, Bexley, Kent.
Secretary: J.W.F. Gaylor
Magazine: *Journal*

Miniature Armoured Fighting Vehicles Collectors' Association,
15 Berwick Avenue, Heaton Mersey, Stockport, Cheshire SK4 SAA.
Secretary: G.E.G. Williams
Magazine: *Tankette*

Scottish Model Soldier Society,
128 Viewforth, Edinburgh EH10 4LN.
Secretary: J.W. Chalmers
Magazine: *Dispatch*

Society of Ancients,
11 King Edward's Avenue, Millbrook, Southampton.
Secretary: T. Bath
Magazine: *Slingshot*

United States of America

The Company of Military Historians,
287 Thayer Street, Providence, Rhode Island 02906.
Secretary: W. Ogden McCagg
Magazine: *Military Collector and Historian*

The Military Historical Society of the USA,
Box 639, Times Square Station, New York 36, N.Y.
Secretary: P.J. Blum
Magazine: *Adjutant's Call*

Military Miniature Society of Illinois,
8116 Niles Avenue, Skohi, Illinois 60076.
Secretary: A.W. Neckerman
Magazine: *The Scabbard*

Miniature Figure Collectors of America,
2555 Haverford Road, Ardmore, Pennsylvania 19003.
Secretary: Blair C. Stonier
Magazine: *Guidon*

National Capital Military Collectors,
P.O. Box 241, Silver Spring, Maryland 20907.
Magazine: *Vedette*

Southern California Militaria Collectors,
1628 East First Street, Long Beach, California.
Secretary: David E. Kay
Magazine: *California Lancer*

Commercial Magazines

Excluding *Tradition*, the following list covers magazines on sale in book stores and newsagents and not produced by societies.

Great Britain

Airfix Magazine
Military Modelling
Model World
Scale Models
Soldier Magazine
Tradition

United States of America

Millastriot
Scale Modeler
Soldier Magazine
The Soldier Shop Quarterly
The Squadron Magazine

Books

As I have said previously, books on military history are very numerous so I shall enumerate only a few of those directly pertinent to modelling and the collecting of models rather than those concerned with uniforms or historical data. Some of these books are known to be out of print (OP) as we go to press, but they should be available through public libraries or through second-hand booksellers specializing in military subjects.

Advanced Plastic Modelling by Chris Ellis. Patrick Stephens, London, 1970.
Handbook for Model Soldier Collectors by Donald Featherstone. Kaye & Ward, London, 1969. Soccer Associates, New Rochelle, N.Y., 1970.
How to Go Plastic Modelling (US title: *How To Build Plastic Model Kits*) by Chris Ellis. Patrick Stephens, London, 1970. Ballantine, New York, 1973.
Making and Collecting Military Miniatures by Bob Bard. Jenkins, London, 1958. Robert McBride, New York, 1959. OP.
Making Model Soldiers by Jack Cassin-Scott. Stephen Hope Books, London, 1974.
Military Miniatures by Peter Blum and Philip Stearns. Odyssey Press, New York, 1964. Paul Hamlyn, London, 1965. OP.
Military Modelling by Donald Featherstone. Kaye & Ward, London, 1970. Barnes, New York, 1971.
Model Soldiers by Massimo Alberini. Orbis Publishing, London, 1973.
Model Soldiers by Henry Harris. Putnam's, New York, 1962. Weidenfeld & Nicolson, London, 1962. OP.
Model Soldiers edited by Col. J.B.R. Nicholson. Belmont-Maitland, London, 1967.
Model Soldiers: A Basic Guide to Painting, Animation and Conversion (US title: *Model Soldier Manual*) by Peter Blum. Arms and Armour Press, London, 1971. Imrie-Risley Miniatures, Copaigue, New York, 1971.
Model Soldiers: A Collector's Guide by John G. Garratt. Seely Service, London, 1965. Fernhill, New York, 1965.
Model Soldiers for the Connoisseur (US title: *Model Soldiers for the Collector*) by John G. Garratt. New York Graphic Society, New York, 1972. Weidenfeld & Nicolson, London, 1973.
Scale Model Soldiers by Roy Dilley. Almark Publishing, New Malden, 1972.
Tackle Model Soldiers This Way by Donald Featherstone. Stanley Paul, London, 1963. Sportshelf & Soccer Associates, New Rochelle, N.Y., 1964. OP.

10: List of Manufacturers

Solid Figures

This is an alphabetical list of some of the more important manufacturers of model soldiers, with a very brief note of their products. Due to the rapid growth of this hobby in the past few years, I am afraid the list will be incomplete, but I hope it will prove to be a basic working guide. (The country of origin appears in brackets beside the company's name.)

Airfix Ltd (UK)
One of the largest manufacturers of military kits in the world, whose products include a limited series of collector's 54mm figures in polystyrene as well as polythene figures in other scales.

Almark Ltd (UK)
Basically a firm publishing military books, Almark is producing a limited range of combination plastic and metal 54mm figures. They are mostly World War II Germans.

Bandai Co. Ltd (Japan)
This is an excellent maker of plastic armoured fighting-vehicle kits, with figures included, in scales from 1/24 to 1/48.

Britains Ltd (UK)
The oldest commercial manufacturer in the world, Britains has been producing military toys since 1893. Present-day products include huge ranges of plastic and a few metal figures which are basically toys, but are useful for conversions. Most of them are within the 54mm scale.

Bugle and Guidon (USA)
A large line of 54mm and 30mm metal figures with an emphasis on US troops and Indians.

Cameo Figures (USA)
These are a limited line of very high-quality 54mm metal military personalities.

Cavalier Miniatures Inc. (USA)
Allan Silk, chief figure-maker, has produced a fine range of 54mm metal figures, including motorcycles and camels. World War I and II are a speciality, but he includes other periods.

Ensign Miniatures (UK)
Made by Major Bob Rowe, this is a superb line of 54mm metal British officers in mess-kit, including appropriate furniture for those in seated poses.

Garrison Miniatures (UK)
This is an excellent range of 25mm metal wargame figures covering most periods.

Greenwood and Ball Ltd (UK)
The original line of beautiful stylized 54mm metal figures by Greenwood is still being produced, but the company has become a consortium producing and distributing the ranges of Garrison, Lassett, Minot, and Sanderson figures.

Helmet Products (UK)
This firm produces 54mm kits in several types of plastic and a mixture of other materials. Its great advantage is that its range includes many British Army figures in periods never before offered in plastic.

Hinchcliffe Models Ltd (UK)
This firm is certainly the most prolific producer of all scales and varieties of metal figures in the United Kingdom. The Ray Lamb 120mm samurai figure, his 75mm range, Frank Hinchcliffe's superb artillery pieces in 54mm and other scales, David Sparrow's 54mm figures, and the vast range of 25mm wargame figures by Peter Gilder comprise one of the finest offerings on the market today.

Hinton Hunt Figures (UK)
This was one of the first firms to start semi-massproduced metal figures, back in the 'fifties. It offers prolific lines in both 54mm and 20mm wargame scales.

Historex (France)
These are by far the most outstanding plastic figures produced in the world today. This firm set the standard for polystyrene 54mm figure kits back in the early 'sixties. Conversion possi-

bilities are limitless although the firm's entire production is devoted to the Napoleonic period.

Imrie-Riseley Miniatures Inc. (USA)
Still one of the world's outstanding producers, this firm offers the best of America's 54mm semi-massproduced metal figures. Its range includes all sorts of unusual subjects from ancient times to the present day, but it concentrates largely on the American forces from the War of Independence to World War II. A few 90mm examples have recently been added to the list.

Lassett Miniatures (UK)
These 54mm metal figures are produced for the Greenwood and Ball consortium by John Tassell, who never stops creating excellent new additions to this range from all historical periods.

Little Generals Inc. (USA)
This is a limited line of 90mm metal figures, covering a wide range of subjects.

Lone Star Ltd (UK)
These are basically toy plastic figures in the Britains category, but again very useful to converters.

Men O'War (UK)
This is a new addition to the list of firms producing 90mm metal figures and, although its range is at present small, the quality is excellent and the figures include very interesting textured bases.

Merite (USA)
This is a line of metal 54mm figures originally produced by Monogram Models, who has since given up all metal production. The range includes some interesting figures, amongst them a Vietcong.

Mignot (France)
Mignot is to France what Britains is to Great Britain. One of the oldest manufacturers of boxed sets of painted metal figures, it is still carrying on that tradition, with French subject matter of course.

Minot (UK)
This member of the Greenwood and Ball consortium produces some excellent diorama figures, 30mm set pieces, and 54mm Napoleonics. All in metal.

Monarch Miniatures (USA)
This is another firm producing quite an extensive range of 54mm metal figures, including a few portraits of obscure personalities such as Emiliano Zapata and Rob Roy McGregor.

Monogram Models Inc. (USA)
This is one of the many large firms producing excellent plastic armoured fighting-vehicle kits which include crew figures, all in 54mm scale. The superb colour photographs and Shep Paine's instructions for painting figures and making dioramas, which are included with each kit, are worth the price alone.

The Old Guard Ltd (USA)
Bill Murray has long been producing fine 54mm metal figures, but he has more recently expanded his efforts and is now exporting. One of his most ambitious recent successes has been a 54mm metal kit of a Stewart tank of World War II. He has recently negotiated a series of deals with European manufacturers which should make a range of American 54mm and 75mm metal figures cheaper over here in return for similar provisions on European miniatures in the States.

Phoenix Model Developments Ltd (UK)
This firm still offers the superb creations of the late Les Higgins and is maintaining his very high standard with its new production of 54mm, 30mm, and 20mm metal figures in a wide range of subjects. It has also brought out an extensive line of metal furniture and household objects as well as some plastic wall-settings, which include panelling, doors, and fireplaces, for the benefit of diorama makers.

Rose Miniatures (UK)
Russell Gamage began producing his very extensive line of 54mm metal figures back in the mid 'fifties and has maintained a standard of quality which has always kept him in the forefront of model production. He was the first to include male and female nude figures for those with conversions in mind, and his historical range has few equals in the business today. He has recently introduced 25mm and 30mm figures to cater to the growing interest in wargames.

Sanderson Miniatures (UK)
Yet another arrow in the quiver of Greenwood and Ball, Cliff Sanderson, in my opinion, is developing into one of the most outstanding miniature figure creators in the world today. The increasing exactness of anatomy in his figures and the perfection of clothing detail are a joy to behold. His more recent releases in the Cavalier and Norman periods are among the finest castings I have ever seen. The figures are metal, and all fall within the 54mm scale; Sanderson has had the very worthwhile idea of turning them out in sets which tell a story.

The Sentry Box (UK)
Miss Edmonds has long been known for her 120mm and 54mm historical figures, some metal and some composition, which can be acquired in either painted or kit form. Included in her range are historical personalities both male and female.

Series 77 Military Miniatures (UK)
As the title indicates, Pat Bird has created a range of figures in a unique scale. Painted and assembled, these metal figures are among the most impressive you can have in a collection, especially if you choose some of those mounted on camels or in ancient Greek chariots. The range is enormous, and his latest products are sets of miniature armour and weapons which make attractive wall decorations when painted and mounted on plaques.

Squadron/Rubin Miniatures (USA)
This is a new series of 54mm metal figures being produced by Ray Rubin for Gerry Campbell of Squadron Shops and it includes World War II pilots and tank crews.

Stadden Miniatures (UK)
Charles Stadden, dean of the creators of 54mm metal collector figures along with Roy Belmont Maitland, is certainly responsible for placing the first high-quality military miniature on the market at a reasonable price. Using a revolutionary new manufacturing method, they started a trend towards semi-massproduced figures in the early 'fifties which has been adopted by almost every model maker since. In my opinion they are more responsible for the birth of the present-day craze for military collecting than any one else. Not only have they led the way but they have trained most of their present competitors in this country. Stadden is a household word in the international military-collecting fraternity. The range is greater than that of any other firm in the business and covers many periods from ancient times to the present day.

Superior Models (USA)
This firm was recognized originally for its 54mm metal artillery pieces and crews, but has recently expanded into the production of a truly superior line of 90mm figures, which are the creation of Lionel Forrest. He has concentrated on figures of the American War of Independence, and the personality and exquisite detail he has incorporated make them by far the best of present-day 90mm production.

Tamiya (Japan)
The leaders in the field of armoured fighting-vehicle plastic-kit production, this firm has continued to improve the quality of the figures which it includes in each kit. In view of the increasing tendency towards placing vehicles in scenes and dioramas, Tamiya has expanded the number of figures in its kits to include more than the vehicle crews. It is now packaging figures for sale separately. The majority of its production is in the 1/35 scale, which is a tiny bit smaller than 54mm.

Timpo (UK)
This is another of the giant toy manufacturers producing plastic figures.

Trophy Miniatures (UK)
Another new British firm producing 54mm metal figures, including two splendid mounted samurai. Its range is as yet quite small but of a high quality.

The Valance Collection (USA)
Produced in America, these 54mm metal figures were created by Major Bob Rowe (mentioned above for his Ensign figures). They are of the same high standard and cover some unusual subjects.

Valiant Miniatures (USA)
Here is a company that must have the largest and most varied choice of 54mm metal miniatures available today. The line includes mythical figures, film personalities, and even a caricature of President Nixon. Many of its military figures are cast in useful action poses.

Willie Figures (UK)
The vast range of 30mm metal figures are the outstanding products of Edward Surén. Their superlative character and detailing make them the finest 30mm figures on the market in my opinion. Edward has recently produced two exquisite military chess sets. He also pioneered camp followers, in 60mm, some years ago.

Flat Figures

The subject of flat figures alone could fill another book like this, and certainly the interest they arouse merits it. But space unfortunately forbids. I can only include a very brief list of some of the more outstanding flats makers in production today: Ruthard Bunzel, Georg Cortum, Dr Werner von Droste, Harald Kebbel, Fritz Manz, Friedrich Carl Neckel, Aloys Ochel, Alfred Retler, Werner Scholtz, and Gerhard Tobinnus.

Acknowledgments

I would like to express my deep gratitude to the many experts in the military-modelling field who have made this book possible. They have been unstinting in their generosity, not only in divulging the secrets of their techniques but also in devoting much of their valuable time to demonstrating for our photographs.

Roy Dilley, President of the British Model Soldier Society and well-known author in this field, has generously donated his time and efforts to reveal his conversion methods using inexpensive figures and combining metal, polythene, polystyrene, and other materials to create superb little gems.

Graham Bickerton, one of the finest artisans on the military-modelling scene today, has very kindly demonstrated his conversion techniques with metal figures and has also taken us step by step through painting a miniature.

The incredibly talented Ray Anderson, whose dioramas have made him world famous, has given us a clear insight into what can be done in the conversion of polystyrene figures, although few of us will ever achieve the sheer genius of his imaginative creations.

My heartfelt thanks must also go to some of the outstanding military-figure painters whose co-operation has not only been a great personal inspiration but who have also done so much to advance the hobby for all of us, experts and beginners. Especially to Donald Burgess for what must be the most comprehensive exposé of painting with artists' oil, to Lynn Sangster on techniques with flat enamels, to Eddie Jones on painting with the new acrylics, and to Shep Paine for his many enlightening comments on modelling, painting, and diorama making.

Nick Larkin contributed his time and materials with unselfish generosity to create our step-by-step diorama and Edward Surén – the master creator of Willie Figures – allowed me into his inner sanctum to give us an idea of the complexities involved in actually making a figure. Jock Coutts of Under Two Flags was a great help in providing kits and models for our photography, and Fred Dell of Wilcox and Freeman was, as ever, generous and helpful.

And, of course, now – as always – I am most grateful to Eugène Lelievrepre and René Gillet of Historex for all their generosity and inspiration throughout my career as a modeller.

Last, but not least, let me thank all of the many talented creators of military miniatures, both those who are my personal friends and those I have yet to meet, whose work has given me so many hours of pleasure and who have provided the basis for one of the most all-consuming hobbies in the world. In the List of Manufacturers I have tried to include you all, but to those I have omitted through ignorance I offer my deepest apologies.

Index

Figures in **bold** type refer to illustrations

Airfix figures **16**, 17, **18**, **33**, **50**, **55**
Anderson, Ray 25, **25**, **26**
Animation 19–28, **19–20**, **22–23**, **33**
 metal figures 19, **19–20**, **22–23**
 mixed mediums 28
 plastic figures 25
Assembly 15–17
 metal figures 15
 plastic figures 17

Balsa wood 28
Bantock, Dr Alastair **8**
Bases 58, **59**, 68
Belts 14, 28
Berdou 9
Bespoke modellers 4, **25**, **53**, **54**
Bickerton, Graham **19–20**, **22–23**, **44**, **50**, **55**
Bird, Pat **19**
Bonding agents 12–13, **13**, 15, **30**
 epoxy 12, 13, **29**
 Heatherbond Plasteel Putty 13, 15
 Humbrol PVC Glue **30**, **31**
 Permabond 12, 15
 Uni-Bond **31**
Books 28, 72, 73, 75
Bridle 44
Britain, William 7
Britains figures 7, 8, 9, **9**, 28, **28**
British Model Soldier Society 8, 28, 74
Brushes 38, 41
Burgess, Ronald **10**
Buttons 28

Cap badges 40
Casting 15, 19, 34, **34–37**
Cavalry figures **9**, 15, **16**, 50, **54**
Cements 13–14, 17
 dichloromethane 13–14
 Mekpac 14, **30**
Chasseur figures **20**, 50
Chess set figures **25**
Chicken wiring 58
Cleaning 15, 50, 68
Cloaks 14
Cluny Museum 6
Collar patch 44
Conrad, Pierre **50**, **54**
Conversion 19–28, **26–31**
 metal figures 14, 19
 mixed mediums 28
 plastic figures 19, 25, **26–31**
Cuirassier figures **7**, 50
Cut-out figures 6

Desfontaine, Josiane 9, 41, **53**
Dilley, Roy 28, **28**
Dioramas 4, **53**, 58–59, **59–64**
Display 68, **68**
 bell-jar 68, **70**
 cabinets 68, **68**
 cases 68, **71**
 lamp 68, **70**
 miniature cities 68, **71**
 shadow box 68
Dragoon figure 50
Drummer figures **17**, **33**, 50, **55**

Egyptian figures 6
Elastolin 9
Emsa, Prince 6
English Civil War figures **53**
Ensign Miniatures figure **10**

Filing 15
Fillers 13, **13**, 14, 15, 19, **22–23**, **27**, **29**, 40
 Milliput **29**
 Squadron Green Putty 14
Flash lines 15, **28**
Flashing 15
Flat figures 6, **8**, 9, **10**, 78
Fordham, David **53**, **66**
Frederick the Great **10**
Fur **27**, 40

Garrison Figures figure **10**
Gaunt, John of 25, **25**
Gilder, Peter **55**
Gillet, René 10, **53**
Glue 15, 58
 Bordens Wood Glue 58
Grenadier figure **44–49**
Gun, 88mm German **67**

Hair **27**, 40, **47**
Hair lines *see* flash lines
Hancock, Winfield Scott **8**
Heads 28
Hilpert, Johan Gottfried 6–7
Hinchcliffe Models figures **10**, **16**, **44–49**, **55**
Historex figures 10, 11, 15, **16**, 17, **17**, **18**, **20**, 25, **50**, **53**
Hollow-casting 7
Horse figures 15, **18**, **19–20**, **22–23**, **33**, 40, 44, **44–49**, 50, **55**, **63**
Hun figure **26**
Hussar figures **5**, 15, **18**, **28**, 50, **50**, **53**, **59–63**, **64**

Imrie-Riseley figures 15, **59–64**

Kennaugh, Mac 33, 50, 55
Kit manufacture 4, 10, **16**, **17**, **18**, 72
Knight figures 6, **6**

Lamb, Ray **10**, **20**, **44**
Lancer figures **19–20**, **22–23**, 50, **53**
Landsknecht **66**
Larkin, Nicholas 59, **59–64**, **66**, **67**
Lassett Miniatures figure **10**
'Lazy Susan' 14
Leggings 43
Lelievrepre, Eugène 10, **33**, **53**
Louis XIII 6
Louis XIV 6
Lucotte 7

Magazines 72, 73, 74, 75
Magonza 6
Mameluke figures **17**, **25**, **55**
Manufacturers 76–78
Medici, Queen Marie de 6
Metal figures 9, 10, **10**, 12, **16**, **19–20**, **22–23**, 28, 39, 50
 lead **7**, **8**
 silver 6
 tin 6, **6**
Metayer 9
Mignot 7, 9
Modelling equipment 11–14
Modrock 58, **60**, **61**
Moulds **35–37**
Murat, Marshal **50**
Museums 4, 72, 73
Musician figure 50

Napoleonic figures **19**, **25**, **26**, **50**, **59**, **64**
Norman Newton figures **5**, 9, 10
Nuremburg figures 7

Oil paint tubes 14

Painting 15, 38–57, **44–49**
 base coat 41
 colour mixing 43–44
 drying times 44
 faces 39–40, **45–47**
 figures 40
 highlighting 44
 shading 40
 skin 43
 texturing 44
 uniforms 40, **47–48**
Paints 38–57
 acrylics 38, 39, 40–41, **44–49**
 artist oils 38, 39, 41–50
 gloss 39
 matt enamels 38, 39–40, 41, 50
 mediums 42
 metallic paints 40
 poster oils 38, 39
 primer 39
 water-based paints 38, 39, **44–49**, 68
Palette 39, 43–44
Pants 43
Paper 28
 tissue **27**
Peaking 40
Pelisse 15, 40
Phoenix Model Development figures **10**, **16**
Piping 44
Plaster 58
Plaster of Paris 58
Plastic cards 14
Plastic figures 9, 10, **16**, **17**, **18**, **26–27**, **33**, 39, 50, **50**
Plastic rods 14
Plastic strips 14
Plasticine 13, 34, **34–36**
Plywood 58, **59**
Pock marks 15
Polyfilla **22**, 58
Polystyrene 12, **13**, 25, 28, 58, 59
Polythene 12, 25, 28, **28–31**
Priming 15, 41
Pyrogravure 11, **12**, **27**, 40

Research 72–73 *and see* Books Magazines, Museums, Societies
Resin 58, **58**, **61**, **63**
Roman figures 6
Ronde bosse figures 7, 9
Roundhead figures **53**
Royalist (English Civil War) figures **53**
Ruddle, John 68, **71**

Sabretache 40
Saddle 44, 50
Sanderson Miniatures figure **10**
Sawdust **62**
Scale **10**, **25**, 58
Scraping 15
Sculpting 19, 34
Seams 15
Series 77 Military Miniatures figures **10**, **50**
Settings 58
Shabraque 40
Societies 72, 73
Soldering 12, 15
Sprues 17, **18**, **27**
Squadron Shops, The 10, 14
Stadden, Charles **5**, 9
Stadden figures **10**
Straps 14, 28
Superior Models figure **10**
Surén, Edward **25**, **34–37**
Sword pommel 40

Terrain 40, **49**, 58, **59–64**
Texturing 40
Thinner 38, 39
Tool manufacturers 11
Tools 11, **11**, 12, **12**, **13**, 15, 19, 38
Trees 59, **62**
Trumpeter figures 50, **63**
Tunic 40, 42, 43
Turpentine 50

Undercoating **44**
Uniform plates 72
United States Civil War figures **8**

Vest 43
Votive figures 6

Wargame figures **55**
Water effects 58–59, **63**
Waterloo, Battle of **55**
Wax 42
Work bench 14
Working area 14, **14**, 59

Picture credits

Most of the photographs in this book were taken by Philip Stearns. The exceptions were provided by Archives Photographiques, Paris (page 6); Connaissance des Arts, Paris (page 7 *left* and *right*); Percy Band Toy Collection, Canada (page 8 *top*); Hamlyn Group Photo Library (pages 56–57); and Keystone Press Agency, London (page 71 *bottom*).